M000033594

BROKEN BREAD

AN ANCIENT LOOK AT THE FIRST LAST SUPPER

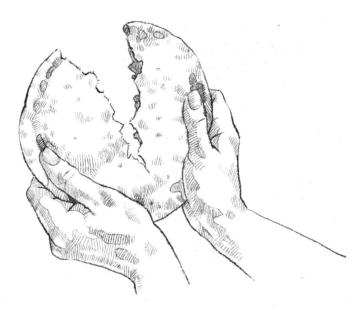

By Jay Richard McCarl

BROKEN BREAD
AN ANCIENT LOOK AT THE FIRST LAST SUPPER

By Jay Richard McCarl

BIBLICAL DINNERS PUBLISHING
P.O. Box 111, Greenwood, CA 95635-0111
Phone: 1-800-240-0927
Web site: http://www.biblicaldinners.org

Cover, Interior Design, and Illustrations by Daniel Cordova

Printed in the United States of America

DEDICATION

For Dr. Jim Fleming, Barbara, Elfie, Irene, and Hannaniah,
who provided the inspiration for the Biblical Dinner presentation
and for this book;

For my friend Gayle Erwin,
who opened my eyes to the nature of Jesus;

And for my amazing wife Kathee,
who has endured so many long nights and tedious absences
for the sake of this ministry...

MENU

(Table of Contents)

The Masterpiece

L ook closely at his face and hands," I instructed my ten-year old daughter Taryn, "They are perfect!" The near life-sized portrait, which hung majestically in a renowned San Francisco art museum, was a true masterpiece. The soft brown eyes of the middle-aged man in the painting were clear and penetrating, glancing left toward the edge of the frame as if he had casually turned toward some ordinary distraction: the rattle of a dish or a dog's bark. His skin was pale and his brow relaxed and carefree, and his face bore a pleasant, grandfatherly look. The chiseled nose was long and straight, his angular cheeks were pleated with the fine furrows of dignity, and his chin bore a handsome cleft. His hands were as fair as his face, smooth and bare, as if he had not worked a hard day his whole life; and his hair, obviously a wig, was as gray as the dusk. The man sat cross-legged and unperturbed, almost bored, in a stiff red chair next to a small table draped with a dark green cloth. The detail was breathtaking.[1]

"Now, Taryn, look at his clothes. What do you see?" and I pointed. She stared for a moment and then squinted. "Daddy, it doesn't look finished!" she whispered loudly, not wanting to make a fuss in the huge, resonant hall. So I showed her what the artist did. The great dignified figure, posing amidst a darkened background, was dressed head to toe in a stately black suit and a silky vest with velvety black buttons. But if you looked away from the noble face and straight at the clothing, all of it was vague, even sketchy, as if the rest of the painting was only blocked in and left unfinished. The shoulders of the man's dark suit were offset by the high back of the red chair, yet both were only a rough suggestion. But if you were not looking for it, you might never notice these remarkable omissions. And that was exactly what the artist intended. He wanted the viewer's eyes to be captivated by the man's face and hands, so he rendered them in amazing detail. But that was all. And unless you knew what to look for, your mind would automatically sharpen the uneven lines and fill in the blank parts of everything he had left out of the painting. He fooled the eyes of his viewers.

As I was explaining the artist's illusion to my now fascinated daughter, I noticed out of the corner of my eye a man standing slightly off to my right. He was also gazing at the portrait and apparently eavesdropping on my little talk (which I was in the process of wrapping up before things became painfully uninteresting). Finally, Taryn and I turned and began to make our way out of the cavernous hall. As we passed through a nearby corridor we could hear (much to our delight) the receding echo of the man's vigorous voice calling his wife and children over to the portrait, telling them of the art lesson I had just shared with Taryn. Their eyes were about to be opened...

Having been an artist most of my life, I have learned that a masterful painting is a marvelously clever thing. And except for many of the more modern abstract works (that often annoy more than enlighten), every good painting tells some kind of story. Whether it is looking into the penetrating eyes of a medieval portrait or examining a hazy landscape chocked with brick homes and leafy trees, the artist is trying to tell us something about life. But like the portrait of the dignified man in black, there is more to see than two hands and a face. It is the background of the picture that sets the stage for the artist's story. Sometimes it appears little more than an unfinished sketch, while in other paintings it is sharp-focused, much tidier than anyone might discern in real life. But the background, regardless of its clarity, is designed by the artist to create a context and add meaning and focus to the true object of their painting (whatever it may be). And unless you earnestly look to see what is going on behind that object, you might never notice that there is anything there at all. And without it, the whole message of the painting could be lost.

The Bible is also a painting. Whenever you crack it open you reveal far more than delicate white pages lined with dense ranks of dull words: you are suddenly plunged into a vast artist's canvas that stretches infinitely beyond the most distant horizon of earthly understanding. Every page is a work of art brimming over with vibrant words, alive and teeming with vivid imagery and meaning; it is a visual feast so immense that all the universe, visible and invisible, can fit neatly within its measureless frame. The great canvas is taut, richly textured, and spectacularly toned, so that every passage becomes a breathtaking vista full of colorful characters awash in the mighty marvels of God. And spread out behind them is an impeccably painted panorama, a lively landscape upon which the often sketchy and unfamiliar doings of its inhabitants burst into clear and radiant meaning. It is the Masterpiece of both time and eternity.

Most people, however, have never read a Bible that looked like that. When they lay open its pages they often feel blasted by a sudden (if not unexpected) flurry of archaic words, uncertain settings, and baffling metaphors that hint of strange and daunting doctrines. So they close the cover and resolve to ask their pastor about it, someday, if they happen to remember.

But the Bible is a surprisingly simple book that was written to very simple people. It eloquently addressed mighty kings, Gentile nations, and scattered Israelite tribes. But it was also written to ordinary herdsmen, farmers, laborers, and women, who, in those days were often illiterate (especially women), and who thought *simply*. Even Hebrew children understood much of the Scripture when it was read to them, because the bulk of the Bible was written like a "Dick and Jane" book. *See Spot. See Spot run. Run, Spot, run.*

It seems God simply wanted people to know Him, and know Him *simply*. And the people of Jesus' day easily grasped His message because they lived in the Bible's towns and villages; not as the heroic characters of a great literary epic but as common peasants turning the same soil as their distant ancestors. They walked the rocky paths of the Land and smelled its pungent breezes; they stretched out their arms under its warm, yellow sun and drank deeply of its cold, dark wells. To them it was just everyday life, but to us who have been removed from their world by the vast oceans of time and distance, the story has taken on the mythical quality of a fairy tale.*

But the lives of those who walked with Jesus were not mysterious, and they left behind countless clues about what it was like to live inside their skin. And if we look at the Bible through their eyes to see life as they saw it, if we learn to care as they did about their customs, the lay of their land, even their weather—all those seemingly mundane details painted in the background—an amazing portrait begins to emerge. The shadowy face of the Man in the old painting flashes into dazzling detail: His eyes suddenly glisten to life, aflame with

---

* Many people have set out on a journey to explore the vastness of the Bible only to find themselves stuck in the deep-cut tracks of three perilous ruts: First, some presume that sounding the immense depths of the Bible is a huge *intellectual* undertaking (it is not); second, because they did not live then and there, it is impossible for modern people to see life through a pair of two thousand year-old eyes (also not true) so that they must therefore spiritualize its message; and third, they can understand the message of the Bible just as well by looking at it through the lens of modern Western thinking. This often results in shabby theology.

a penetrating and irresistible knowledge of the human heart; His vague demeanor sharpens into crystal clarity, revealing a focused face radiating with perfect grace and truth and justice. The shape of the Man's linen robe is rendered only as a sketchy suggestion, but it transports our eye's attention to His rugged hands and feet, which hold the deep wounds of iron nails and an unrelenting love. He is a Man like no other, and against the towering background of creation's measureless mural He stands Supreme. He is God's eternal self-portrait. He is Jesus[2]

One final thing: the Painting is not some lofty, snooty parlor piece, which simple people could no more appreciate than a young child could enjoy a good algebraic equation. Children do, however, love pictures, and so do I, and the Bible is packed with them. We just need a little help so we can understand what we are looking at.

And that is what this book is all about.

Let me show you...

INTRODUCTION

You are Invited!

You are almost there. The sinking sun is now low on the horizon; you have been hiking all afternoon over the rocky Judean countryside in shabby leather sandals, and your feet hurt. You had set out from your humble stone house in the cool light of a clear morning with walking stick in hand, toting a small stuffed with your one change of clothes and a few dried morsels for the journey. But the pleasant morning sun flared into a blazing knife, piercing even the close-wrapped shade of your linen turban. Now, after a long and toilsome day traversing hard uneven paths with scarce shade and too many flies, the last few drops of moisture sloshing in your water bag have turned warm and ill-tasting. Your traveling rations of raisins, roasted wheat grain and stale barley bread are nearly gone. But it does not matter now, because *you are almost there.* You have been invited to a feast!

Not many days ago you were scratching shallow furrows in the bleached soil of your tired land, preparing to sow some meager seeds that would produce a life-sustaining crop for you and your family. Suddenly, you notice a stranger striding briskly up the steep path to your house. He is an older man, not poor, and dressed with a certain modest dignity; and you recognize him. He is the chief servant of a good and faithful friend.

"Peace be upon you!" he greets. "Are you the one my master is seeking?"

"I am!" you reply, unsure of his intentions.

"My master will be hosting a great feast that will last many days, and he has sent me to invite you. You are to be his guest of honor! The feast will be on the first full moon of the next month. You will be there? Yes? Peace!" Then almost as quickly as he appeared, the man is gone...

Time passes neither slowly or quickly, for you live in an age without clocks or datebooks. All you know is that many days have passed since the man invited you. Then, not unexpectedly, the same faithful servant, dusty and tired from his journey, appears a second time at your door. And you knew he would come, because tradition demands that a good servant repeat his invitation to make sure he did not accidently summon to the feast an enemy of his master.

"Don't forget! My master's feast begins soon—you will be there? Yes? Peace!" You offer him water, raisins, and some bread, which he gratefully receives. You both recline in the warm shade of your olive tree where you eat and catch up on the local happenings. After much too short a visit the servant graciously excuses himself.

"I must be about my master's business. Peace!" And he is gone.

"He will return soon," you say to yourself, "and then I shall go with him!"

The shining moon waxed nearly full last night, and you slept restlessly in the anticipation of the coming day. "The servant should be here soon!" you say to yourself. The morning sun climbs ever so slowly until it stands high above the eastern hills. There is a wisp of dust churning in the distance. Could it be him? Then, as if magically materializing out of a shimmering mirage, you see him coming up your path, walking briskly.

"Peace be upon you!" he declares with a broad smile and a raised right hand. "The fatted calf has been killed and prepared, and remember, you are my master's honored guest!" A great honor indeed, and a very special meal it will be. And you must attend, for once the feast is prepared it must be eaten or that marvelous setting will all go to waste, and that would be an evil and insulting thing.

Your bundle is already packed for the grueling trek. You set aside both plow and trade—there are no time cards to punch—and you disappear with the servant down a narrow lane bordered by squat walls of chunky rock shaded by an occasional overhanging olive bough. As you follow, the servant constantly turns and urges you to come, tugging at you and beckoning you to pursue him to the feast, as if you needed such urging. But smiling, you know that it is just his master's honorable way of impressing your neighbors and making you feel most welcome.

You maneuver your way through a flock of shaggy, complacent sheep crowding the lane, but today your mind travels far ahead of your feet. "I will have supper tonight: bread, wine, fresh fruit, honey…and meat!" Not the scanty meat of dried, salted fish, and not your usual daily ration of runny vegetable broth and lentils, but real meat, which you have not eaten since that last Passover. Even then it was rationed out to the many hungry inhabitants of your village: a single roasted lamb, prepared according to the Law of Moses, then torn up and mixed into a plain peasant's stew. Not much meat, and it had to feed many mouths. It was the best you or anyone in your village could manage because you are all poor, and a lamb is costly. But now you are going to a feast, and tonight you will eat tender beef with brown bread made of real wheat, and wine! That cup of joy!

You both pause under a shady mulberry tree to swallow a mouthful of cool water from your leather flasks. Your eyes brighten, the urging resumes, and now you quicken your pace…

PART ONE

Greetings

I am waiting at the gate of my house, crouching on a low stool, dressed in my finest celebratory robes. The land and the air are beginning to cool as the warm day settles into a soft twilight. A thin breeze begins to blow, and it feels good on my face, mercifully refreshing after a long busy week of hard preparations for my feast. "They should be arriving soon," I remind myself. I have long anticipated a hearty visit with my old friend.

I glance across the fading horizon, straining to see someone approaching with a familiar gait. A silhouetted figure suddenly emerges from behind a nearby grove of shadowy olive trees. "That's just the herdsmen's son—where is my servant?"

Then, cresting over a distant hill glowing with the stark, sidelong rays of the setting sun, another figure appears, and then another. "There he is! But where is my friend? Ah! Here he comes!" And I arise and stand in the polite, customary manner of my people and await their arrival. I hear the echo of my servant's ceaseless urging of my friend: "Come! Come to the feast! We are almost there! See? There is my master—he awaits you!" And I do. And now at last we stand face to face, my friend and I. He is sweaty and dusty, thirsty from the long journey, and his feet are hot and tired. But he is home, for my house is now *his* house.

I am so glad he is here. And I greet him…

CHAPTER 1
Shalom

"Shalom. Shalom Aleichem!" And in the gladness
of our reunion we happily bestow upon each other
this marvelous, albeit customary pronouncement.
But it is no hollow cliché. This warm welcoming
is rich with meaning—in fact, it brings something
wonderful into our lives and to our visit together,
something from God Himself.

"Shalom aleichem!" I say to you, and I mean it.

"Aleichem ha-shalom!" you heartily reply, and we
revel in our time together...

To your average English-speaking American, this greeting sounds a lot like someone trying to clear their throat. In the robust Sierra Nevada foothills of California where I have lived the greater portion of my highly Westernized life, local bull-riders will tip their sweat-stained Stetsons in token respect and drawl a colorful "howdy." On the salty boardwalks of the Southern California beaches you might hear a piping, "howzit goin', dude?" as you leap aside to dodge a runaway skateboard.

We have all grown up with all kinds of manners and means to greet each other. "Hi." (I wonder what that means?). "How are you?" (do I really want to know?). "Hello!" (huh?). "Good to see you…" (this greeting sometimes makes a liar out of me). Need I go on? This is why I like "Shalom." It means "peace", and the ancient greeting was even better: "Shalom Aleichem," "peace be upon you," and it was a blessing.

The Bible tells us that Jesus greeted His frightened, anxious disciples with "peace be upon you" no fewer than three times during the week following His resurrection. Late on the very day of His resurrection, His disciples had locked themselves inside a Jerusalem house, fearing that the same men who railroaded Jesus to the cross would soon be pounding on their door.

Suddenly and miraculously Jesus materialized in their midst, uttering the cheerful greeting, "Peace be upon you!", and He meant it. This, of course, terrified them. But stripping his sleeves and side to reveal His shocking wounds, He blessed them a second time: "Shalom aleichem!" as if to say, "Fellows, you don't need to be anxious anymore, it's really Me, I'm with you now, and My peace is yours!" Then He blessed them, He breathed on them, and, as the Apostle John told us, they were finally overjoyed.

More than any other people on earth, the Jews seem to understand the power of blessing. They knew that God was a God who loves to bless. In the Book of Numbers God gave to the priests of Israel a marvelous blessing to bestow upon His people:

> The LORD bless you
>> and keep you;
> The LORD make His face shine upon you
>> and be gracious to you;
> The LORD turn His face toward you
>> and give you peace.[3]

And then God even put His own Name on the blessing because He was most certainly willing and able to do it.

A blessing is a mighty thing. A story is told of a cantankerous man named Lonnie Ray. He was a chronically unemployed drunk who had (to the townspeople who knew him) proven himself a completely useless member of the human race. One day, while in a particularly self-deprecating mood, he placed an order with a local leather crafter for a custom belt engraved with the scornful words, "God D--- Lonnie Ray." The leather crafter, a committed Christian, could not bring herself to carve the condemning phrase into Lonnie's belt even if she felt he might have completely deserved the awful sentiment, and she told him so. "Then put on any blankety-blank thing you want!" Lonnie retorted. And she did: she decided to inscribe the belt with the words, "God *Bless* Lonnie Ray."

That afternoon he returned to the shop to collect the item. The leather crafter nervously handed Lonnie the belt with the altered sentiment. Instead of being pelted by a salty outburst (as was anticipated), she was greeted with a surprising reaction: Lonnie burst out laughing. "I love it! 'God *Bless* Lonnie Ray'! What a great joke!" He paid her his money, put on the belt, and paraded himself through the town and his usual haunts of bars and other seedy places, proudly showing off what he considered one of the funniest jokes of all time. The cry of, "God Bless Lonnie Ray" soon became the jest of the whole community.

"Look! Here comes Lonnie! God *Bless* Lonnie Ray!" And he would laugh and hoot right along with the rest as both stunned passersby and drunken mockers chimed in on the blessing. The joke had brightened the overall countenance of the seaside hamlet, and it was on the verge of becoming something of an institution when it unexpectedly died out after just a few short weeks. In the course of that time Lonnie had inexplicably stopped drinking, got a steady job, and started behaving like a civil human being. God blessed Lonnie Ray.

A coincidence? Not likely. A blessing is a mighty thing: it is a grace from God that changes things, something that He has even given to His people to bless others in His Name. "Peace be upon you" is one such blessing, and if I happen to bestow it on you, will God not get personally involved?

The Bible is full of blessings that originate with, and ultimately return to the God who loves to bless. He blesses us and gives us blessings to give to others, and then He blesses them, too. "Shalom Aleichem" is just such a blessing. I meet

6 | Greetings

you and bless you with my greeting, and God does the rest, bestowing on you whatever it is you might need that only He can provide.

So, may His peace rest upon you and your whole household; and may your friends and neighbors also receive of the graciousness of God, especially because you have blessed them, too.

That is how it works. Be blessed…!

Shalom Aleichem.

CHAPTER 2

I Salute You

The fingertips of my right hand arc upward to gently touch my chest near my heart, and then fluidly, almost elegantly ascend to touch my lips, then my forehead. With a subtle flourish, I now offer to you my open, upraised palms punctuated by a slight, modest bow of my head; and I do all this while conferring upon you those marvelous words of blessing, "shalom aleichem…"

In today's practical world we might let slip a chuckle at such a poised gesture cast in our direction. After all, this mysterious motion looks as though a second rate Hollywood screenwriter had invented it for a low-budget Arabian adventure. Of course, it was anything but. You see, I have saluted you.

One day Jesus called together His disciples to present them with a new project: they were to go out in pairs among the villages of Judea, preaching to the people that the kingdom of

God was near. He then bestowed on them the authority to heal people and cast out demons, and gave them an abundance of strict instructions they were to observe during their brief and speedy mission. "I am sending you out like lambs among wolves," He told them; and then He said, "Do not take a purse or bag or sandals; and *do not greet anyone on the road...*"[4]

Wait a minute. Do not greet anyone on the road? Jesus was certainly exclusive, but to impose such a command on His own evangelists smacks of rudeness. Can you picture it? You are toiling on a mundane project under the shady eaves of your stony house when you notice two men rapidly approaching along the narrow lane to your village. They are walking briskly and purposefully and their brown robes are weather-worn and stained. But they bear none of the other usual accoutrements expected of travelers, not even a wooden staff, and they are certainly not from around these parts.

"Ah, strangers!" you muse. It has been a dull day—in fact it has been a dull year, and some pleasant conversation would be most welcome. Your ancient tradition of hospitality engages. With a cheerful "Shalom!" you politely greet the approaching visitors, but you are met with a peculiar silence.

You say to yourself, "Perhaps they did not hear," so you repeat your hospitable welcome: "Shalom! Peace!" More silence. Now passing quickly by, the strangers confer upon you a determined, if not grateful glance, yet still they do not reply as they disappear down the rocky lane. "Now that was rude!" you mutter to yourself, bewildered by such a brazen insult. "Wherever they have come from, it must be a terrible place full of vulgar people!"

That was the thinking of that day. Hospitality on any level in the ancient Middle East was both revered and mandatory. To not respond politely to another's greeting was considered particularly bad manners. To ignore another's greeting altogether was a coarse insult. But was this what Jesus intended when he told His disciples not to greet anyone on the road?

In the original language of Luke's Gospel, the word that has been translated into English as "greet" meant "salute," and a salutation was a greeting that was accompanied by a special gesture. When you welcomed a stranger with a cordial "Shalom," it was required in those days to answer with an equally polite reply. Everyone did it, and all the time.

However, if you *saluted* someone—met him with a certain customary gesture—it was a signal that you would sit down with him, partake of his hospitality, and talk for a while. *A long while*. In fact, if someone offered you this friendly token and you responded in kind, you would be expected to sit down in the shade with them and socialize *for a day or two*, perhaps even longer. So, Jesus gave His disciples wise instruction: "Do not 'salute' anyone on the road. Be polite, but I do not want you to linger or be delayed in this mission of compassion. Heal, bless, preach, but do not remain too long because the fields are ripe, and you will not have much time to harvest." But what was this gesture?

The Bedouins are a mysterious and amazing desert people: nomads, who, for thousands of years have wandered the vast, bleak deserts of the Middle East herding their flocks from mountain to glen in search of seasonal pastures. Today these durable people are mostly Muslim, but their conversion to Islam was a recent development, one that occurred a mere sixteen hundred years ago. But for uncounted centuries they have traversed wastelands crisscrossed by caravan routes, foreign traders, invading armies, and migrating civilizations. Hence, they have had constant and intimate contact with the exotic cultures and traditions of countless tribes and long-vanished empires. They are accidental collectors of customs, a living time capsule of some of the most ancient goings-on and habits, and most important of all, they are Semitic. And for as long as anyone can remember, they have greeted each other with a particular gesture that rooted itself in the traditions of virtually all the Semitic peoples living in and around ancient Judea. That is until recently. The modern world has taken its inevitable toll even on the sturdy Bedouins, and the gesture is beginning to fade into history.

But for now, and even after thousands of years, it is still here, and for good reason. Like the sign language of deaf people, gestures are able to transcend almost all language barriers and changes. Early on, Israel and Judah were conquered by Philistines, Midianites, Assyrians, Babylonians, Medes, Persians, and Greeks, to name a few. By the time of Jesus' ministry they had lived under the tyranny of Rome for almost a hundred years. But even so, the people still knew how to say "hello" to almost anyone anywhere, and in a respectable manner that was as modest as it was honoring.

So I salute you: I highly esteem you and rejoice to sit with you and enjoy your company, whether it is under the shady boughs of a sycamore or breaking bread at my table. And as I offer you my salute, here is what I am saying to you:

First of all, the gesture always begins with my *right* hand, because welcoming you with my left hand would be a demeaning insult. Why? We will get to that later.

Then, with the fingertips of my right hand, I gently touch my heart, as if saying to you, "With my heart, I love you..." In fact, since I am your host, you are now partaking of my legendary Middle Eastern hospitality, which means that if for any reason you were threatened, I would gladly trade my life for yours.

I now lift my hand to touch my lips, telling you, "With my lips, I honor you…" In other words, no matter what language I speak, I will only say good and honorable things about you.

Raising my hand to touch my forehead, I now say to you, "With my thoughts I worship you…" But wait a minute— that sounds like some old pagan idea, perhaps even a type of idolatry. It is not, of course, nor could it be, or the Israelites (or even the Muslim Bedouins) would have outright refused to practice it. So, what, then, did it mean?

Simply this: the people of that ancient world knew absolutely nothing about one of the great sacred cows of our modern world, *self-esteem*. In fact, this recent popular trend would not have entered even their wildest imaginations, except perhaps in the way kings expected to be treated. They did, on the other hand, understand and practice the idea of *others*-esteem.

The emphasis that the modern world and even Christianity has placed on self-esteem is a curious thing in light of the fact that the Bible never really addresses it. Even more, it seems to run quite contrary to almost everything Jesus taught concerning the very foundations of ministry.* Even the Apostle Paul commanded the Philippians, and for that matter all Christians, to "Do nothing out of selfish ambition or vain conceit, but in humility consider others better than yourselves."[5] He further confessed to the church at Corinth that he boasted—*bragged*— about the things that revealed his *weaknesses*. Even about the Lord Jesus Christ Himself, the apostle wrote,

> *Who being in very nature God, did not consider equality with God something to be grasped, but made himself nothing, taking the very nature of a servant, being made in human likeness. And being found in appearance as a man, He humbled Himself and became obedient to death—even death on a cross! Therefore God exalted Him...*[6]

* This includes Jesus' teaching concerning "the greatest commandment," or loving your neighbor as yourself. It has often been taught in recent years that Moses (and Jesus) meant that in order to effectively love your neighbor, you must first learn to love yourself. But this is a late twentieth century idea, and not at all in concert with any known Biblical theme taught by Moses, Jesus, or the apostles. I highly recommend the book, "The Jesus Style" by Gayle D. Erwin for a thorough examination of the others-centered ministry of Jesus.

This does not sound at all like the pop-culture line of today's world, which may explain why modern people seem so needy of personal affirmation. Remember, it was Jesus who reminded His disciples that, "He who finds his life will lose it, and whoever loses his life for my sake will find it."[7]

A fascinating story is told of the great American psychiatrist, Dr. Karl Menninger. Following a provocative lecture on the subject of mental health, one of his students asked the esteemed therapist, "Dr. Menninger, what would you advise a person to do if that person felt a nervous breakdown coming on?" Dr. Menninger's answer was not quite what the class expected. The students seemed certain he would explain how one should go and seek out a good psychiatrist who would painstakingly walk them through their anxiety and set them on the road to recovery. Instead, the doctor simply told the student, "Lock up your house, go across the railway tracks, find someone in need, and do something to help that person." *Others* esteem.

We have all endured long, empty hours when we have felt glum, isolated, and even depressed. And it is in times like these where we tend to grasp for some gold-plated approach to feel better and think more highly about ourselves than our gloomy situation might dictate. But all too often our pursuit of adding to *self* and esteeming our *selves* is like chasing a rainbow: it looks so colorful and lovely, so perfectly filling of our need, and we run and run to take hold of it. But having all the substance of a mirage it lingers just beyond our most determined reach, with its pot of gold hopelessly hidden in the land of the leprechauns.

But there is another path, one that has, perhaps, a few more rocks and roots growing out of it. But this bumpy, narrow lane leads us to a clear stream where we can drink ourselves full. This is the path of esteeming *others* as better than ourselves, for it is when we add to the lives of *others*, bless *others*, that we find our value, our fulfillment, and our meaning in life. Jesus taught His disciples all about this beautiful irony. It was called "The Sermon on the Mount,"[8] and with His entire earthly life He showed us how it worked.

"With my thoughts I worship you—I esteem you as greater than myself." It appears the ancients had it right all along.

Finally, I open both my hands to you, showing you that there is nothing in them for me to harm you. At the same time, I conclude with a slight bow, as if to say, "I humble myself before you. I am your servant."

The gesture is a language without words, a picture that paints my good intentions toward you, my honored guest, foretelling of the gracious nature of our visit together. And the entire fluid motion is accomplished in the time it takes for me to bless you with the words, "Shalom Aleichem."

Now *that* is a greeting.

CHAPTER 3

"Greet One Another With…"

I place both my hands on your shoulders, and you place yours on mine. We know what to do, for we and our most distant ancestors have practiced it. I pull you in close and kiss you on your right cheek as you do the same to me. Then I kiss you on your left, then again on your right. Just a slight peck on each cheek three times, but it is more than enough to tell you that I accept you and welcome you…

Y ou want us to do what?" There was a startled look of disbelief and terror on their faces, as if I had suggested to my audience that they all go and throw themselves off a bridge. "That's right. I would like you to kiss one another, men with men and women with women: hands on each other's shoulders, one peck on each cheek, three times, please. Now, greet one another with a holy kiss." Of course this is one of the many ancient customs which I reintroduce during my Biblical Dinner presentation. On this particular evening, however, the room was packed with Americans, and despite their rather freethinking cultural leanings, *they just don't do that sort of thing*.

Unfortunately, in the rest of the world this American cultural dread is the exception, not the rule. On the other hand, almost every nation, tribe, and people that happened to have been influenced by the Roman Empire or the Middle East will greet with a kiss. In fact, in many cultures where is it staunchly inappropriate for men and women to kiss or show affection in public, to *not* greet a guest or friend with a kiss would be equally unbecoming, if not insulting. In South America people will frequently greet with one peck, in Europe it is with two, in the Middle East and parts of Asia, three. In parts of Africa, though not an actual "kiss," many will press their cheek against yours twice. And they are not just being polite. They are indeed showing proper affection for you, but even more, they are initiating your visit together with an intimate act of loving acceptance. It seems to me that most Americans are really missing out.

Of course, in the days of the Bible it was somewhat common for people to greet with a holy kiss, and the Apostles even encouraged the churches to do so no fewer than five times.[9] But if they already greeted in this affectionate way, why, then was it so famously emphasized in their Writings? The answer is almost too simple when you think about it. The Apostles seemed to have wanted this kiss to show off Christian love.

People did not always greet with a kiss every time they met. The apostles Peter and Paul, therefore, encouraged the churches to kiss and kiss often, apparently as a very public and proper display of Christian love, especially under the scrutinizing gaze of a suspicious world. Such an affectionate expression of peace underscored the great declaration of Jesus when He told His disciples "by this all men will know that you are my disciples, if you love one another."[10]

Now, the Bible mentions many kisses, but two of them are especially notable, and neither could be more radically different. One is often spoken of as the most infamous act in human history, when a holy kiss of peace became the diabolical instrument of Jesus' betrayal by his disciple and friend, Judas Iscariot. The other kiss, however, is not nearly as well known, but it is perhaps far more significant. It is the story of a father who kissed his son…

One day, Jesus was dining and speaking with a gathering of notorious "sinners." Also listening was a pack of Pharisees who were appalled that a prominent rabbi like Jesus would openly eat with such people. So Jesus told them all a parable. It was a story about a father who had two sons, the older of whom was obedient and respectful, the younger, rebellious and self-absorbed.

One day the younger son coldly announced that he had had enough of life at home. "Father, I wish you were *dead* so I wouldn't have to wait around to get my part of your inheritance!" This was the essence of his complaint, and it was heartbreaking and painfully insulting to both his father and his whole village. According to Jewish law, as punishment for such an outrage the father had the right to drag his son outside the village and have him stoned to death. Instead, he decided to divide his vast fortune between the two sons. Not long after, the younger packed up his belongings and his ill-gotten wealth and journeyed to a far country where he freely indulged his wildest and most wicked whims. But as is so often the case with youthful extravagance, the money soon ran out and he was left stranded and alone in a remote pagan land with no means and no hope of home. To make matters worse, a famine broke out in the land and he began to starve. He had burned his last bridge and now he was really *stuck*.

In desperation, the frantic son took the only job anyone would offer him, feeding carob husks to a herd of evil-smelling pigs. But his unscrupulous master refused to pay him, and he began to drool over the vile pods he was tossing to the un-kosher herd. This was a bitter plunge for a good Jewish boy, and now his whole life had come to slopping hogs in a hostile country as a starving slave. It was then he woke up.

"The least of my father's own servants have it better than this!" he said to himself, "I'm going home." But the young man had slammed many doors on his way out—what would he say to his father? "I will just have to tell him the truth," he relented, "I will say, 'I am no longer worthy to be called your son, hire me on as one of your servants.'" And off he went.

"While he was still a long way off," Jesus continued, "his father saw him and was filled with compassion for him; he ran to his son, threw his arms around him, *and kissed him.*" The reckless son had forsaken his family and was lost, but his father loved him still, and day after day he anxiously scanned the horizon, aching for the miracle of a happy homecoming. Then one day, there emerged in the deep distance a ragged silhouette, approaching, and walking with a familiar gait. "It's him! I know his walk! My son has returned!"

Hurriedly gathering up between his knees his great patriarchal robe, exposing his naked legs, the old man began to run toward the tattered figure. Despising his own dignity, he fell on his son's dirty neck, hugging him tight and long, and many tears flooded the old man's tired, strained eyes. Then loosening his embrace he held his son by the shoulders with a firm and loving grip, and he kissed him, affectionately, first on the right cheek, then the left, then again on the right. It was an adoring declaration, a fervent and passionate monologue without words, yet it spoke more than any tongue could ever tell.

It was a holy kiss, and like a clean, new sword it pierced straight through the heart of both father and son, mingling together the blood of brokenness with the wine of limitless compassion.

Then, there was the other kiss, the kiss of Judas. It was also a kiss of peace. But this time it was bequeathed by the son of perdition[11] upon the sinless Son of God, plunging Him into treachery, torture, and a horrific death. It is both strange and beautiful that the kiss conferred by the father upon his prodigal son was the same kind of kiss, but bestowed instead upon a reckless, rebellious boy. Neither of these young men deserved what such a kiss delivered to them.

Ironically, the kiss of Judas unwittingly paved the way for Jesus' death on the cross for the salvation of you, me, and everyone who would ever believe in Him. On the other hand, the kiss of the prodigal's father remains a wondrous reminder that God is waiting, even for the lost and destitute, even if it was his or her own doing. Even if the prodigal is you.

If you have been away, come home. When you do, He will be waiting, and He will run to you, fall on your neck, and greet you, too; and it will be with a kiss of peace—with a holy kiss.

Here is the rest of that marvelous story…

But while he was still a long way off, his father saw him and was filled with compassion for him; he ran to his son, threw his arms around him and kissed him.

The son said to him, "Father, I have sinned against heaven and against you. I am no longer worthy to be called your son."

But the father said to his servants, "Quick! Bring the best robe and put it on him. Put a ring on his finger and sandals on his feet. Bring the fattened calf and kill it. Let's have a feast and celebrate. For this son of mine was dead and is alive again; he was lost and is found." So they began to celebrate.

Meanwhile, the older son was in the field. When he came near the house, he heard music and dancing. So he called one of the servants and asked him what was going on. "Your brother has come," he replied, "and your father has killed the fattened calf because he has him back safe and sound."

The older brother became angry and refused to go in. So his father went out and pleaded with him. But he answered his father, "Look! All these years I've been slaving for you and never disobeyed your orders. Yet you never gave me even a young goat so I could celebrate with my friends. But when this son of yours who has squandered your property with prostitutes comes home, you kill the fattened calf for him!"

"My son," the father said, "you are always with me, and everything I have is yours. But we had to celebrate and be glad, because this brother of yours was dead and is alive again; he was lost and is found."

– Luke 15:20-32 –

PART TWO

Warmth and Welcomings

It was a long and tiring journey. The afternoon sun was overly warm and the path rutted and rocky, but you are here! My house is splendidly prepared for you, the great table is set, and my servants are waiting. And that means hospitality and *feasting*…

"Come in, come in!" I urge you, and I lead the way. We kick off our sandals and step cautiously over the stone threshold, slipping into the cool shadows of my cheerful home. I call out to my servants, "Bring a stool for my friend, and water for his feet!" And with my command I begin to lavish upon you, my honored guest, four delightful gifts of hospitality. But they are no token display of my good manners; they are *expected* of every good host.

In fact, to *deny* you these four friendly gifts would be an enormous sin, and you would quickly conclude that I was both rude and insulting. Even more, if I held back these gifts you would automatically assume that my whole village must also be full of ill-mannered people just like me. In Biblical times people often judged others by the group because of the failings of a single individual (it appears not much has changed over the centuries). So, for the sake of the good reputation of my village, let alone my own honor, I would take great pains to smother you with these gifts and make you feel as welcome in my home as you would in heaven itself.

People still judge people by the group. But because Christians are called to live holy lives in this world (a truth which most everyone understands), they tend to be scrutinized more sternly than others. "Christians are hypocrites," a man complains. "Are you certain of that?" I ask. "Absolutely," he replies, "The car that cut me off on the way to work this morning had a "Jesus" sticker on it. That's a hypocrite in my book!"

Hmm. This sort of thinking is, of course, unfair by any standard, and it is certainly not limited to ill feelings toward the Christian community. That Christians should live perfect lives, however, is also a false expectation often piled upon believers by the unbelieving world. Unfortunately, Christians sometimes embrace their own false expectations as well.

Have you ever seen the old bumper sticker, "Christians aren't perfect, just forgiven"? Perhaps you last spotted it rocketing past you, affixed to the rear panel of the car that nearly ran you off the road. Yet many Christians expect that just because God forgives them, everyone else should be quick to do likewise. "After all, we are all human and we make our share of mistakes." True enough, but even though it is certainly wrong to judge a group by the errant actions of a single individual, with Christians, things are a little different. According to the Bible, the world *has permission* to judge a Christian *as Christian* according to his likeness to the One he professes to follow.[12]

Let me put it another way. The Book of Acts tells us that the followers of Christ were first called *Christians* in the ancient city of Antioch.[13] But in those days "Christian" was not a kind word. It meant "little Christ," and the person who coined the expression intended it as an insult. But never was a more appropriate label pinned on believers. *Little Christs*. This is the "group" whom their own Master gave blanket permission to the watching world to judge, not by the failures of its members, but by their individual resemblance to Him.

People still judge people by the group, and until Christ returns to rule and reign, this will remain a fact of life on earth. And as long as Christians live in this world, their likeness to the Lord and Savior they profess to follow will constantly be inspected. And rightly so, because a Christian, though human, is still commanded to walk as Christ walked *in everything*.

If you are a Christian, the last time you went to the store to buy your groceries your checker met Jesus when she met you. The question is, how honest was her meeting with Him? Did she experience a grouchy, impatient

Jesus, or did she meet a Jesus who looked upon her with kindness and understanding?

When you found yourself stuck in heavy traffic last week, did the other drivers encounter an aggressive, irritated Jesus, or one who offered some gracious road courtesies that made their grueling drive home a little more tolerable? This is tremendously important, because despite the injustice of weighing others by the group, people will do it anyway. And like it or not, each individual Christian represents the entire village. How we Christians treat others—*any* others—can spark the praise or reproach of other believers everywhere... *and of Christ*.

Our gifts and courtesies will always represent the entire village. It may not seem fair, but it is still true. Perhaps this is why the Apostle Peter told Christians to "offer hospitality to one another without grumbling."[14] The reputation of the whole village—and the Master—is riding on it.

Chapter 4

The First Gift: Clean Feet

Your feet hurt. You have been plodding all afternoon over rocky, uneven trails in your worn, flat-footed sandals. The dust is heavy; flocks and herds have recently trodden the same path, and there is no one to sweep it clean. You pass through a compact village with narrow, grimy streets that smell bad. Someone leans out of a dark window and spills the rancid contents of a filthy bowl into the narrow lane. You step wide to avoid the unpleasant mess, but cannot, so you slog through the repulsive residue. This is just the way things are, and you pay it no real heed. You have a fine feast and warm fellowship waiting, and such routine things need not deter you.

Your long path ends at my stony threshold, where your soiled sandals are shed and deposited outside my door. You are ushered into my house, and the air smells of fresh-baked bread, roasted meat, incense, and new straw. I seat you on a low, stout stool. It feels good to sit down under a shady roof.

"Come now," I call out to one of my servants, "Bring water for the feet of my honored guest." The servant has stood in waiting, and he comes over quickly. Kneeling down, he gently cradles your right foot and slides a brass basin under it. He is dressed scantily: bare-chested with a large linen towel wrapped around his waist, and he does not appear happy. Supporting your foot, the servant bathes it with cool water from a clay pitcher, rinsing away the filth and tiredness of your journey. He begins to scrub with his bare hands the dirt and grime from the sole of your foot and between your toes, being careful not to let it touch the fouled water collecting in the basin. He rinses your foot a second time, and then wipes it dry with the towel around his waist. Now the servant begins to wash your other foot. It feels luxurious and refreshing—a marvelous delight for a footsore guest. All is bliss!

Except for the footwasher, that is…

In the days of the Bible, footwashing was considered the worst job a man could do, and you can well imagine why. It was a truly disgusting notion to scrub someone's feet with your own bare hands, knowing full well the sort of muck and mire they had collected from the roads. Even more, because of the offensive nature of their job, the footwashing servant or slave was regarded as the lowest form of human life on earth. And if I, your host, had no servants or slaves to call upon, tradition would demand that I personally wash your feet. You can imagine how humbling it would be to me to offer such a service, and how honoring it would be to you.

But there is something else about feet. Perhaps you have seen news footage of formal meetings between Arab dignitaries and Western diplomats. If you have, you may have noticed that the diplomats are usually seated in large, overstuffed chairs, appearing a little clumsy and somewhat uncomfortable. But they are just being careful, trying hard *not* to do something that almost any Westerner would do without thinking: they are keeping their legs and ankles carefully *uncrossed*. In fact, both feet usually remain flat on the floor because they do not want to risk an international incident by accidently exposing the bottom of a shoe. Really. To do so, even by accident, would be a monumental insult, because to the Middle Easterner the bottom of your foot is the filthiest part of your body, and to expose it to another, especially on purpose, would be an outrage.

During one of my Israel tours I escorted a small group of friends to Jerusalem's colossal Church of the Holy Sepulcher, a huge and ancient edifice believed by many to be built atop the place of Jesus' crucifixion and resurrection. The central feature of the enormous church is a small rock-hewn tomb jealously preserved in the great rotunda, a relic revered by Christians throughout the centuries as the actual grave where Jesus was buried and rose from the dead.

My friends soon slipped into a long queue of Nigerian pilgrims who were waiting patiently for a look inside the tomb, but since I had visited this place many times (and my tried feet were beginning to protest), I decided instead to look for a place where I could sit and read my Bible. I soon located a familiar wooden bench, hard but welcoming, wedged into a stony alcove across from the entrance of the extravagantly adorned Sepulcher. I was just beginning to enjoy the momentary reprieve from our grueling tour of the Old City when loud and incoherent shouting startled me out of my reading. It was directed at a dark-haired European woman seated to my left.

In front of her stood a tall, black-bearded man clad in a long gray robe and capped with a brimless stovepipe hat. He was a priest, one of the custodians of the Holy Tomb, and he was very unhappy, railing at the woman and pointing. Neither of us recognized the strange language of the angry priest, and she made motions to him to signify her bewilderment at his umbrage. Realizing that she could not understand, the man curtly gestured, crossing, and then uncrossing, his rigid arms. Then he pointed at her *feet*. I looked down and saw that she was wearing an elegant pair of black, low-heeled walking shoes—but her ankles were *crossed*. Her relaxed and modest pose had allowed the bottom of her feet to angle ever-so-slightly upward, *exposing the soles of her shoes in the direction of the Tomb*.

To this Middle-Eastern custodian of Christianity's most sacred relic, such a display was wholly irreverent, if not blasphemous. She began to understand. The woman uncrossed her ankles, placed her feet flat on the floor, and looked up at the irritated priest. His countenance remained stern, but he lifted his palms in the direction of the woman, as if to say, "Now you know. Do not let it happen again." Then he turned and walked brusquely away, disappearing into the congested entrance of the tomb.

Have you ever wondered what Jesus meant when he said of His betrayer, Judas Iscariot, "He who shares my bread *has lifted up his heel against me…*"?[15] What a revelation this was of Judas' mind towards Jesus!

And can you now imagine being the household servant who was required to wash the feet of your master and his guests; that *you* are the one commanded by your master to handle and cleanse the most unclean part of another person's body, and that those parts represented the very essence of vile insult? And perhaps worst of all, you are painfully aware that only the lowliest servant or slave performed footwashing, because no respectable master would assign such a disagreeable task to anyone above the status of a dog.

In a time where everyone walked, it was your feet that touched the world, and the world was really *dirty*. The grime of the earth stuck and reeked: it needed to be scrubbed off and rinsed away, and when it was, there was refreshing. And somebody had to do it. Such a man was truly the lowest of the low.

You will need to remember this later…

CHAPTER 5

The Second Gift: Cold Water

A mouthful of cool water—how wonderfully refreshing it sounds! And your dry mouth agrees. Your journey was long and hot, and it has been hours since you squeezed the last few drops of moisture from your old leather water bag into your small wooden cup. It tasted lukewarm and stale. But now you are under my roof, and you are my honored guest.

Your feet have been washed, and you are already feeling greatly refreshed. Stepping away from the little stool, you now sit back on your heels on fresh, comfortable mats, layered across the bare floor. As you situate yourself, your eyes suddenly brighten and you smile, because you hear the cheerful sound of fresh water splashing into a cup. Another servant approaches, and he is carrying a small tray laden with dripping water cups and a wet, clay pitcher.

And now I offer you my second gift of hospitality: a cup of cold water. "Ahh," you sigh with delight, and I hand you a cup from the servant's tray. You smile and drink deeply of the cool refreshment. But your gladness of the gift runs deeper still, because you understand that this cup means more than a mere thirst-quencher. You have just been *received*.

Never underestimate the value of water in the Middle East. In Israel, it does not rain much, and the region has a long history of devastating droughts. But when it does rain, unless you have some sort of clever system to capture and hold the water, it disappears quickly. Israel is very rocky—in fact, much of Israel is blanketed with vast ribbons of white limestone buried just beneath the shallow surface. When it rains, the water quickly penetrates the thin soil, sheeting over the limestone where it vanishes quickly westward towards the Mediterranean Sea or eastward, into the arid Syro-African Rift Valley. There is, of course, the Jordan River and the Sea of Galilee. But unless you are a lowland farmer (and not a mountain herdsman), you would probably not live near either of these cherished water sources.

Water is precious, and for me to present you water is to offer you something of great value to both of us. More than that, I will offer you a cup of *cold* water. You see, even though it may be the first century, I own something like a "refrigerator," and it works rather well. Have you ever noticed how cool it feels when rubbing alcohol or even gasoline touches your skin? Neither is actually cold, but because of its chemical make-up, when it touches the warmth of your skin it evaporates very quickly. It is this rapid evaporation process that actually cools things off. The same is true of ordinary water, and the ancients came to understand this. On a hot day they would fill a plain, unglazed earthenware jug with water, then bathe the outside of the jug with more water. As the moisture on the outside of the vessel evaporated, the water on the inside would naturally cool down. A first century refrigerator! I could then pour for you a refreshingly cool cup of water even on the hottest of days. And I will, because it is a gift of hospitality, and you must be made to feel welcome and received.

Received? Absolutely. In this modern age, if you came to visit me at my house in California, I would open the door for you and invite you in, ask you to sit down, and, of course, offer you something to drink. This is good manners, and it is respectful. But for someone living in ancient Israel, offering a cup of cold water was a matter of *receiving* someone, and to withhold it was to inform your guest that you did not like him, and that you even *reject* him.

Remember what they thought about water? It was far more than a polite thirst-quencher, it was precious and valuable. And to offer a cup of cold water to someone was to declare their great worth to you, and that you approve of them, take them by the hand as it were, and receive all that they are and all that they bring with them. Here is how this worked...

You are walking through the narrow streets of a neighboring village when you notice up ahead a large throng of people blocking the way, all of whom are straining hard to hear someone who is speaking. You are immediately curious and begin to press your way through the packed crowd until you are standing next to two plainly-clad strangers. One of them is speaking boldly about how the Kingdom of God is near, and someone next to you points and excitedly tells you, "That one healed my son—he must be from God!" It is an amazing scene: some of the people are openly weeping with joy, a few others are scoffing and sneering, but none appear indifferent to the speaker's fiery words.

Suddenly, as if struck by lightning, you find that you, also, are cut to the heart by his penetrating message. He concludes his sermon and the crowd begins to disperse, but you linger because the things he said have marvelously moved you. You want to thank him, but no! You want to do much more than that—you want to somehow show him that you embrace him along with his astonishing message. But you have nothing to give him, no way to adequately express your gladness at his wonderful words.

Then you remember: "I have water! I will give him a drink of my water!" And you rummage through your sack for a small wooden cup and hastily fill it with water from the goatskin pouch hanging at your side. It is still early in the day and the water is still cool. "Here, please drink from my cup!" you eagerly tell the man. He smiles and blesses you and drains the cup. And he, too, is blessed, for by offering the disciple your water, you have not merely quenched his thirst, you have taken him by the hand and received him. What is more, you have embraced his message, and even the One who sent him.

Listen to Jesus' parting words to His disciples as He was about to send them off on a short, speedy mission:

He who receives you receives me, and he who receives me receives the one who sent me. Anyone who receives a prophet because he is a prophet will receive a prophet's reward, and anyone who receives a righteous man because he is a righteous man will receive a righteous man's reward. And if anyone gives even a cup of cold water to one of these little ones because he is my disciple, I tell you the truth, he will certainly not lose his reward.[16]

It is remarkable how closely Jesus identified Himself with His disciples. So much so, in fact, that He told them that God Himself will reward anyone who welcomes them, for by doing so they have also taken *Him* by the hand and received *Him*.

Perhaps you remember the story of Jesus' encounter with a Samaritan woman. As He was travelling through the region of Samaria, Jesus sat down next to a deep well, hot and weary from His journey. A short time later, a woman, a despised outcast even among her own people, approached to draw some water. Jesus then did something that broke all the rules: He asked her for a drink.

Her response seemed rude, but it was in perfect keeping with their traditions: "You are a Jew and I am a Samaritan woman. How can you ask me for a drink?" Jews and Samaritans disliked each other intensely, and for this woman to give Jesus a drink, even at His request, signified her taking His hand in hospitality. Suddenly her prickly question makes more sense. But then Jesus did an even more astonishing thing: He offered *her* a drink—of *living* water, which really got her attention.

There is a lot of confusion about the subject of *living water* in the Bible, so much in fact, that today, if you were to ask a Christian what it was, they may have a difficult time coming up with a solid answer. But to the people of the ancient Middle East, living water was an obvious and much sought-after thing. *Living* water was water that was moving, like a babbling brook or an artesian spring bubbling up out of the earth. It was *alive*: streaming and splashing over rocks or surging up out of the ground; it was fresh fallen raindrops running together and flowing into swift, small rivulets or raging torrents. It was clean, aerated, and pure; it invigorated and refreshed, and it was wholesome. It was nothing like the stagnant, ill-tasting waters of a deep, dark well or a cistern. That water was dead. Jesus offered the Samaritan woman water that was uplifting, thirst-quenching, and life-giving. Of course He used her understanding of *living* water as a spiritual metaphor, and at first the woman believed He was being entirely literal. And she would have been right in doing so.

She implored Him, "Sir, give me this water so that I won't get thirsty and have to keep coming here to draw water." In other words, "Show me where it is." But Jesus was offering her so much more: "If you knew the gift of God and who it is that asks you for a drink, you would have asked him and he would have given you living water…Everyone who drinks this water will be thirsty again, but whoever drinks the water I give him will never thirst. Indeed, the water I give him will become in him a spring of water welling up to eternal life." She was sinful and immoral, a lost lamb wandering amidst the unhappy ruins of a wasted life, and Jesus knew it. Still, He urged her, "Ask *Me* for a drink, and I will receive *you*. Take My cup and drink My gift, for I welcome you with *living* water, which will flood your soul with eternal life!"

This despised Samaritan woman needed to allow Jesus to *receive* her, and He was extending His hand to her, wicked sinner though she was. The story does not tell us if she ever gave Jesus any water, but it did not really matter, because it was not about what she could do for Him. Salvation is always about what Jesus has done for us. He came to us and He came *for* us; He died the death we deserved to die because of our sins, and He rose from the dead to eternally live for us as the mediator between God and all humanity. He did it all.

That is the nature of His loving grace: it cannot be bought, earned, borrowed, or coerced—it can only be received. And it is a cup of *living* water, cleansing, refreshing, and life-giving, offered freely and hospitably to all sinners, no matter how wicked. He also holds this cup out to you. "Take it," He would say to you, "and drink deeply. Let me take you by the hand and welcome you, for in My Father's house there is life. Come, enter into My hospitality."

Refreshing, isn't it?

Here is the rest of the story…

The woman said to him, "Sir, give me this water so that I won't get thirsty and have to keep coming here to draw water."

He told her, "Go, call your husband and come back."

"I have no husband," she replied.

Jesus said to her, "You are right when you say you have no husband. The fact is, you have had five husbands, and the man you now have is not your husband. What you have just said is quite true."

"Sir," the woman said, "I can see that you are a prophet. Our fathers worshiped on this mountain, but you Jews claim that the place where we must worship is in Jerusalem."

Jesus declared, "Believe me, woman, a time is coming when you will worship the Father neither on this mountain nor in Jerusalem. You Samaritans worship what you do not know; we worship what we do know, for salvation is from the Jews. Yet a time is coming and has now come when the true worshipers will worship the Father in spirit and truth, for they are the kind of worshipers the Father seeks. God is spirit, and his worshipers must worship in spirit and in truth."

The woman said, "I know that Messiah" (called Christ) "is coming. When he comes, he will explain everything to us."

Then Jesus declared, "I who speak to you am he."

Just then his disciples returned and were surprised to find him talking with a woman. But no one asked, "What do you want?" or "Why are you talking with her?"

Then, leaving her water jar, the woman went back to the town and said to the people, "Come, see a man who told me everything I ever did. Could this be the Christ?" They came out of the town and made their way toward him.

Meanwhile his disciples urged him, "Rabbi, eat something."

But he said to them, "I have food to eat that you know nothing about."

Then his disciples said to each other, "Could someone have brought him food?"

"My food," said Jesus, "is to do the will of him who sent me and to finish his work. Do you not say, 'Four months more and then the harvest'? I tell you, open your eyes and look at the fields! They are ripe for harvest. Even now the reaper draws his wages, even now he harvests the crop for eternal life, so that the sower and the reaper may be glad together. Thus the saying 'One sows and another reaps' is true. I sent you to reap what you have not worked for. Others have done the hard work, and you have reaped the benefits of their labor."

Many of the Samaritans from that town believed in him because of the woman's testimony, "He told me everything I ever did." So when the Samaritans came to him, they urged him to stay with them, and he stayed two days. And because of his words many more became believers.

They said to the woman, "We no longer believe just because of what you said; now we have heard for ourselves, and we know that this man really is the Savior of the world."[17]

CHAPTER 6

The Third Gift: Dripping with Love

Your feet are now squeaky clean and your burning thirst has been happily satisfied, but for you, the best part is at hand. You peel the sweat-stained turban from your head—the cool air feels good as it breathes through your hair. And now I step behind you and kneel down. You hear a slight crack, the breaking of something small and brittle, and all at once the air is filled with a fragrant aroma that gladdens your heart. You close your eyes in anticipation, for I am about to lavish on you the gift you desire above all the others. I anoint your head with scented olive oil.

There are many examples in the Bible of people being anointed with oil, especially kings and priests as they were initiated into their weighty titles. But anointing someone with oil was also a much-anticipated gift of hospitality.

In most churches, the Biblical tradition of anointing a sick person with oil usually involves an elder placing a tiny drop of olive oil on his fingertip then dabbing it on the forehead of the recipient. They have now been anointed, and the elder begins to pray for them that they might be healed. But as your host, this is not the sort of anointing I have in mind for you, and you would hardly be honored by such a meager display of attention. Instead, I crack open the lid of a small clay flask that is filled to the brim with some very special olive oil that is reserved for my most important guests. The oil is scented like flowers or other exotic spices; its bouquet is pleasant and uplifting and subtler than the overwhelming aroma of expensive, heavy perfume. I pour out over your head the entire contents of the flask, soaking your hair; it runs down your forehead and onto your beard, dripping carelessly onto the shoulders of your robe.

Now, as you read the description of this ample gift it is possible you are thinking, "What a mess! Do you know what that would do to my hair? And watch out! Don't get any of that on my clothes—it will leave stains!" As you know, in today's hygienic world, walking around with lanky, dripping hair and oil-spotted clothing might be considered completely *unattractive*, if not disgusting. But two thousand years ago you would have thought much differently, because such an anointing was not only a tremendous honor, it was even regarded as highly fashionable.

Do you remember how precious water is in the Middle East? The Jewish people were far more fastidious than most ancient peoples, but they still lacked an abundance of water with which to regularly bathe. After a few days or weeks (or longer) without a dip in the Jordan River, Lake Galilee, or even a mikveh,* people would get pretty ripe. Of course, this was just life in those days, and you got used to it. But now you have been anointed with my oil and your hair feels shiny and clean, because to you, this is what clean feels like. And more than that, there is now a wonderful fragrance filling the air, which is emanating from you, for I have made you the source of all things good and pleasant in the room. I have not just anointed you, I have beautified you in the presence of my entire household.

But there is more, and it is perhaps the best part of all. After I have poured this wonderfully aromatic oil all over your head, I step behind you and begin to massage it into your scalp. This may sound odd, but that is only because it involves touching a friend's head, which to your average modern Westerner is considered a rather intimate thing. But have you ever had a scalp massage? It is truly one of the great luxuries in life. And imagine having beautifully scented oil massaged into your scalp by strong fingers after a long, tiring journey. This is truly the gift of hospitality where you would urge your host, "Keep going! Don't stop!" Ahhh…this is the life!

Days from now, when you finally leave my house to return home, people along the roads will glance your way, seeing your oil-drenched hair and spotted robes. But you know that they will only be impressed, and perhaps even a little envious. And they will be thinking, "There goes someone who is loved!"

* A *mikveh* was ceremonial cleansing pool in which the ancient Jews would immerse themselves before performing a solemn ritual or task.

For the Lord takes pleasure in His people;

He will beautify the humble with salvation.

– Psalm 149:4 –

CHAPTER 7

The Fourth Gift: Just the Right Atmosphere

As you bask in the luxurious afterglow of your aromatic anointing, I attend to one final gift of hospitality: I sprinkle a pinch of incense on a few hot lumps of charcoal burning on a stone base in the corner of my room. You are my guest, and I want everything to be just right for your honored visit to my humble house; and, frankly, before you arrived it smelled like most houses did in those days: it reeked.

Before you entered, you doffed your dirty sandals outside my door and stepped over the threshold into my room. *Threshold.* Have you ever wondered about that word? Today we usually picture it as the doorway through which a new bridegroom will carry his beautiful bride on their wedding night, or the seal at the base of any door leading into a modern house. But to the ancients, a *threshold* did just that: it held thresh. It was a stone ridge across the base of the doorway leading into a house that held in a thick layer of matted weeds and straw strewn atop the dirt floor. *Thresh.* And it was there for good reason.

My animals are my wealth, especially if I am poor. They give me and my family good things and provide for my meager income: wool and milk from my goats and sheep, and eggs from my chickens. I would certainly not eat my livestock, I could not afford to; and neither could I afford to lose them. In those days Judea was a perilous land in a much wilder world, and the dark nights were full of thieves and dangerous predators like lions, bears, jackals, hyenas and leopards. So, if I wanted to protect my investment, I could spend long, nervous nights standing watch over a corral, *or* I could instead secure them in the safest shelter I knew—my own living room. And now perhaps you understand why I need all that thresh—and the pinch of incense. The thresh caught what the animals left behind, and the incense blunted the intense odor.

If, on the other hand, I were a wealthy man, living in a large villa with a red-tile roof and polished mosaic floors, I would still welcome you with incense. I might own many flocks and herds, and I am rich enough to pay to have them guarded by night. But my windows have no glass, only shutters, and the animal aromas of my sizeable herds would still invade the sweet ambiance of my feast. So, I honor your visit with fine incense, which will fill the room with an exotic and exquisite atmosphere. For as a guest in my house you will receive only the very best.

There is an excellent example of this arrangement in the Bible, one that stood out to the people of that day but has since been clouded by our more modern view of life...

One day, as Jesus was speaking to a crowd that had gathered around Him, He told them a parable about a woman who had lost a coin in her house. "Does she not light a lamp," Jesus asked them, "sweep the house and search carefully until she finds it? And when she finds it, she calls her friends and neighbors together and says, 'Rejoice with me; I have found my lost coin.' In the same way, I tell you, there is rejoicing in the presence of the angels of God over one sinner who repents."[18] When you read this parable, perhaps you thought, "How poor the woman must be! If she does not find her coin, she will not be able to buy food or perhaps pay some terrible debt!" But that is not what the people heard as they listened to Jesus.

In those days when a woman married, it was customary for her to take ten silver coins from her dowry, bore a hole in each one, and sew them around the hem of her veil. It was a rich symbol of her marriage and of her own great worth. In fact, her coins were like a wedding ring. In Jesus' parable a bride suddenly discovers that one of her coins is missing, and to her dismay it has dropped off somewhere in her living room. The room is not large, but it is dark, and it was built that way because flies do not like the gloom. But the floor is also blanketed with a thick layer of matted thresh (for obvious reasons), and her coin has apparently fallen into the heap.

Frantic, she lights the flaxen wick of a small, clay oil lamp and begins the painstaking task of mucking through the deep, murky carpet of soiled straw. Hour after hour she searches, one small area at a time, clutching the lamp as she sifts inch by inch through the grimy layers. Then, in the flickering lamplight, she spies a silver glint among the decomposing weeds, and she snatches it from the mass. "The coin! Here it is! I have found you!" Considering her great effort and the unpleasantness of her search to recover the coin, is it any wonder that she called her friends over for a celebration?

Like that coin, we, too, were once lost, fallen into the dark, murky jumble of a world fouled by sin. But Jesus loved us so much that He refused ever to stop seeking for us—searching and sifting inch by inch—until we were found by Him. And then He, like that woman, threw a *party*. And now He has stitched us, His lost coin, securely onto the veil from which we had fallen, where we are now put on shining display for all the angels of God to see—as His glory, His worth, and His joy.

Hallelujah!

CHAPTER 8

Just the Beginning...

Welcome to my home and to my hospitality! You have been personally summoned, welcomed, blessed, kissed, washed, refreshed, anointed, massaged, beautified, and honored. The room is right: the air itself is rich with the aroma of roasting meat, exotic incense, fresh-baked bread, boiled leeks and vinegar, and there is a slight tinge of oily smoke from burning wicks and torches. The floor is layered with fresh mats and pillows, and a large low table, blanketed with colorful coverings, is warmly lit with flickering olive oil lamps. Just outside you hear the bustle of busy people: sounds of water splashing and clay pots clacking, the rhythm of stone grinding grain, hands slapping bread dough, and someone humming a song.

And the food! There is food all over the table: purple grapes and rose-red pomegranates, ripe apples and yellow-rind citrons, apricots, plump figs, and sweet brown dates! There are baskets of almonds in the shell, cakes of raisins, plates of spices and salt, bowls of golden honey, and there are great round sheets of pale bread singed at the edges and still smoking hot from the griddle. Cups, jugs, and stacks of small clean plates are waiting on the table, and there are servants hustling in and out of the room carrying in still more food! Other guests and family members now begin to enter and greet, their faces shining with delight and they gesture and bow in your direction and recline with you at the table.

Your mouth begins to water, but it is not yet time to eat. As your host, there are still a few things I must do before we begin, but they will not take long. After that we will eat my feast together; what a time we shall have!

And we are just getting started...

PART THREE

Come to the Feast

W e are just getting started, but first we must prepare for another journey, and this time it is not just to a different village. We are off to visit a distant kingdom in another age, travelling far into the future to look in on the dining room of a fifteenth century Italian chapel.

More food?

No, not exactly.

But what possible connection could there be between a first century feast in Judea and a fifteenth century chapel in Italy?

None, whatsoever...

CHAPTER 9

The First Last Supper

Leonardo da Vinci was truly the quintessential Renaissance man: he was a brilliant scientist, inventor, mathematician, musician, botanist, architect, engineer, anatomist, and writer. But above all else, Leonardo was renowned as an extraordinary artist, and especially so, having painted the two most recognized and beloved paintings in world history: the subtle *Mona Lisa*, and the magnificent *Last Supper*. A mural almost nine meters wide and five tall, *The Last Supper* is painted nearly life-sized in a fresco style (water-based paint applied to wet plaster) on a wall of the dining hall of the Chapel of Santa Maria delle Grazie in Milan, Italy. It is an ageless depiction of Jesus seated at a dinner table with His disciples on the night of His infamous betrayal, and it is unlikely that there is a household anywhere in the western world that does not possess a copy of it.

For more than five hundred years The Last Supper has stood upright and solid, enduring disastrous earthquakes and wars, surviving a door being cut through its base, and even weathering layer upon layer of oily, sooty smoke residue from ages of lamps and torches. But it would not be able to tolerate an experimental painting technique that Leonardo applied while creating the great masterpiece, and it began to deteriorate in his own lifetime. Even so, its muted splendor and understated passion continue to stir the hearts and imaginations of all who gaze upon it. "Glorious!" people will exclaim. Others will tearfully cross themselves and kneel at the wonder of its spiritual majesty. It is moving, breathtaking, brilliant, superlative in every way—*and wrong.*

Leonardo was truly a genius for the ages, but he was no theologian. However marvelous his painting may be, it does not at all resemble the *historical* Last Supper, and the beauty of *that* is in the details (as you will see later on).

The original Last Supper was a Passover Feast, which, to the Jewish people was their most important ceremonial meal. It had to be specially prepared according to the commands God gave to Moses, and it was repeated every year at about the same time. As the Last Supper began, the Bible tells us that Jesus *reclined* at the table with His disciples (we will talk about that in the next chapter), where He told them, "I have eagerly desired to eat this Passover with you…" Since Jesus said plainly that this special meal was indeed a Passover feast, then da Vinci's illustrious depiction of the celebrated event has some significant problems.

For instance: according to the law of Moses, the Passover was always to take place at night, but as you look at the painting you will see the hazy glow of a blue afternoon sky

Jesus. Leonardo painted Jesus and the disciples seated on high stools at a long, elevated table that was draped with a clean, white tablecloth. But the ancient Jews never ate their meals at a long *or* elevated table, nor did they sit on stools or chairs to dine; those were reserved for kings and queens. And where would they ever obtain such a large piece of fine white cloth for a table covering, even if it was for a very special occasion?

Jesus, who would have been the host of the feast, is painted at the exact center of the table, but the host of any sort of feast would never be found at such a vulnerable location. If you look *under* the table, the disciples are all still wearing their sandals, which would have been very bad manners. The main course at every Passover meal was roasted lamb, but it could be that Leonardo did not have a taste for lamb, because he painted fish instead. And one of the most important ceremonial items on any Passover table was the crepe-like unleavened bread. But Leonardo seemed to think that some nice round Italian dinner rolls would be better, so he added these as well. Leonardo da Vinci's *The Last Supper* remains among the greatest masterpieces ever painted, but it is simply dreadful theology.

The ancient Jews would never eat a meal like we do today, or even like Leonardo did during the Renaissance. Peasants would typically eat right on the ground, kneeling on dirt floors, woven mats, or flagstones. The poorest peasants would often gather around a clay cook pot bubbling on a bed of hot charcoal, where together they would dip shreds of flat bread into a meager broth or stew. In fact, they rarely ate meat, perhaps only once a year during Passover, unless they could somehow afford to buy some dried salted fish.* Those who were more prosperous would typically dine in a room of their house, reclining on mats, pillows, or ornately woven carpets** and eating their meal from bowls and platters served on a low table or on the floor in front of them.

---

* The poverty of those days was staggering, so much so that the clothing you were wearing when you woke up is the clothing you would wear for the rest of the day—and every day—until it completely wore out. Think about it: where do you go to find a new tunic? Would you walk down the road to shop at the local boutique? And even if such a place existed, how would you pay for a new garment? You would have to make it yourself, but where would you get the cloth? You would have to make that, too, or find something to trade for it. Simply put, peasants did not have a closet or trunk full of changes of clothing; they simply wore what they had on until it completely wore out.

** The carpets of those days were not at all like the exotic Persian rugs of the Hollywood Biblical epics. In fact, the soft, fuzzy style of Persian rug is a much more recent development. The *kilim* variety of rug, however, which bears a colorful woven, needlepoint look, became somewhat common about two hundred years before Christ. This would have been the most likely sort of floor covering upon which the wealthy would have reclined.

But by the time of Christ a new tradition had been introduced in Judea, and it was a custom that Jesus seemed to have honored. The rabbis decided that once a year every Jew, even the poorest, was to eat one meal like the rich, and that occasion was the Passover. Why? The Passover Feast was established by God to remind the Jewish people of many wondrous events, both past and future, but it especially celebrated their miraculous deliverance from hundreds of years of backbreaking bondage as brick-makers in Egypt.

You remember the story: led by Moses the Hebrew slaves escaped Egypt, fleeing through the watery walls of the parted Red Sea on dry ground. As the last few stragglers scrambled up the banks of the far shore, the Israelites stared in astonishment as the sea crashed down upon the deadly chariots of Pharaoh's vengeful, pursuing army, drowning them under the crushing maelstrom. Now they stood breathless on the flowing shoreline, gazing back in wonder across the impassible gulf toward the land of their former slavery. For the first time in almost four hundred years, they were *free*. And as the rabbis of Jesus' day rightly concluded, if you were *free*, you were *rich*. "So as you eat the Passover," they would tell you, "remember your freedom, remember that you are *rich*."[*]

The Last Supper Table

But what did a rich man's meal look like, and how could a poor peasant afford such a thing? The solution was actually

---

[*] This, of course sounds very American, and it should, for it is from *Judeo*-Christian values that we have acquired such cherished principles.

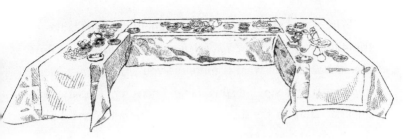

quite clever: you would dine around a rich man's table, a structure that almost anyone could improvise or, if need be, rent. In ancient Judea, a rich man's table was an item of furniture derived from an elegant Roman design, which they called a *triclinium*.* A triclinium was a three-sided, "U" shaped table that usually stood just inches off the ground** and around which the diners would recline (think about the word: *tri*, meaning three, and *cline*, suggesting a couch on which you would recline).

As guests would arrive, they would take their positions around the outside edges of the table (and in some more elegant settings, *on* the table) with no one sitting inside the "U"—that was an area reserved solely for the busy servants who would wait on the diners. This distinctive "U" shape is what made it a rich man's table, proudly declaring that you were well off enough to afford servants or slaves. And there is one more subtle detail about this table that you will need to remember later: the open end of the "U" always faced the entry door…

---

* It is a strange irony that Judeans would use a Roman design to celebrate freedom at their greatest Jewish feast, considering that the Romans were their oppressors and they despised them.
** In even earlier times or among the very poor, a triclinium "table" might be a simple woven mat laying flat on the ground

Why is any of this important? Namely this: this table—a triclinium—*is the most likely shape of the historical Last Supper table*. And what is more (as you will also see later), knowing the shape of this table opens up a marvelous understanding of the things that were said and done during the course of that remarkable evening.

But why is this style of table believed to be the kind around which Jesus and His disciples ate the Passover? Aside from it being a tradition of that age, there are a few good clues.

There once lived a man named Titus Flavius Josephus, who was a first century Jewish-Roman historian. Born just after the time of Christ, Josephus wrote two great works, *The Antiquities of the Jews* and *The Jewish War* that were not only historical accounts, but also a treasury full of insights into the background of ancient Judean life. In one of his accounts he happened to mention a special type of room: an exclusive dining room used for elegant feasts and furnished with a triclinium table, which he referred to as a *kataluma*. To Judeans, a *kataluma* was a guest-room, usually an upstairs part of a personal residence or public lodging place (like the "inn" which was too crowded to house Mary and Joseph when they arrived in Bethlehem), but the meaning also retained its more fashionable connotations. This is clue number one.

Clue number two is found in the Gospels of Luke and Mark. It was the morning of the Last Supper, and Jesus was about to dispatch Peter and John to begin making preparations for the evening's Passover feast. Luke tells us what happened next:

Then came the day of Unleavened Bread on which the Passover lamb had to be sacrificed. Jesus sent Peter and John, saying, "Go and make preparations for us to eat the Passover."

"Where do you want us to prepare for it?" they asked.

He replied, "As you enter the city, a man carrying a jar of water will meet you. Follow him to the house that he enters, and say to the owner of the house, 'The Teacher asks: Where is the guest room, where I may eat the Passover with my disciples?' He will show you a large upper room, all furnished. Make preparations there."

They left and found things just as Jesus had told them. So they prepared the Passover.[19]

As you might have already guessed, the word Luke used for "guest room" was *kataluma*, and the description of its large size and complete furnishings implied it was no ordinary guest chamber.

Clue number three is revealed in the answer to this question: Who was the man with the water jar, and why did Jesus specifically want to eat the Passover at his house? Passover week always found Jerusalem packed with pilgrims, and some accounts put the number at more than a million worshippers. They all came for the Feast, they all needed a place to celebrate it, and the people of Jerusalem were always happy to accommodate them, *for a price*. As the pilgrims began to arrive, residents would rent out their homes and guest rooms to the visitors, earning them a decent wage in a short time for very little work. Whether the situation was prearranged or not, Jesus knew what was needed for a location, and He knew where to find it.

"A man carrying a water jar will meet you," He told Peter and John. But carrying water was women's work, so what sort of man would be lugging around a water jar? Some scholars suggest that this was a secret sign for Peter and John to follow, pre-arranged by Jesus to secure the peace and privacy of an evening destined to end in betrayal and desertion. The answer, however, may be much simpler: the man with the water jar may have been an Essene—a member of a monastic Jewish sect. As a monk he would have been celibate, and with no women in the sect, he would have had to carry his own water. And the Essenes of Jerusalem are believed to have occupied a very secure compound at the south-west corner of the walled City, a safe location full of homes with lots of guest rooms to rent—*katalumae*, and all were furnished for a successful Passover celebration. Today the Jerusalem neighborhood is called Mt. Zion, and although it now sits outside the walls, there is an ancient tradition that says the Last Supper happened *right there*.[20]

This is what a rich man's table looked like, and it is the best picture of the real Last Supper. But what if you were so poor that you could not possibly afford to rent a kataluma or to improvise a triclinium table? To fulfill the tradition of the rabbis, all you would need to do is lay blankets out on the ground or perhaps scratch its shape in the dust and recline around it. You see, even if you were *very* poor, this custom was invented to remind you that real wealth is found elsewhere, in that wonderful, intangible thing called freedom.

This is our wealth, too, and it is not so base as to be merely political or national in its essence. It is a liberty which transcends every idea and aspiration of men, one which can be celebrated even under Roman (or any other) oppression. Though one may be confined to a cell, a police state, or a broken body, this freedom is a festival for the soul, for you have been freed for all time and eternity from the hard fetters that chain a man's soul to his own shame, and worse, to an irresistible, final sentencing. The one who rejects the freedom Christ offers is also free—free to go his own way, but also to an inescapable end of his own design. Apart from Christ, like Scrooge's ghostly partner Jacob Marley, he remains bound by a great and ponderous chain of his own making. That is true poverty.

So rejoice! Celebrate your freedom, for it was bought and paid for by the death of Jesus, who was our Savior, our Moses, sent by God to set His people free. The blood of Jesus, the Passover Lamb of God, was painted on the doorposts and lintel of your house where the angel of death saw it and *passed over* you, and would not harm you. Your Deliverer has led you out from the land of your slavery to sin and through a miraculously parted sea. It was there where your enemy, that relentless foe of guilty condemnation, was drowned in its watery depths.

And now He stands with you on the shore of a new land, a new life. There is no turning back, in fact, there is *no way* back, for that road lies at the bottom of an impassible sea. And there is no more raging army that can overtake you and destroy you. The one whom the Son sets free is free indeed!

Celebrate your freedom, for you are rich with an abundance the likes of which no tyrant or earthly lack can ever take from you. Recline now at the rich man's table and partake, for you are home, and you are free. *Indeed!*

CHAPTER 10

The Reclining Position

T he warm sunny day has finally melted into a cool evening, and the first glittering stars have awakened in the dusky sky. A wholesome breeze begins to whisper through small windows, swirling across the expanse of the homey room, gently brushing your face.

Ah! You are feeling the warmth of your welcome. And as your eyes blink in the dimness, there before you, nearly filling the room rests a glimmering triclinium, splendidly illuminated with the yellow light of many flickering olive-oil lamps. The table is richly laden with a rainbow of fresh fruits, bowls brimming with hard-shelled nuts, golden honey, pungent vinegar, salty broth, dark olives, and pale hummus; there are platters of meats and vegetables, baskets full of sweet dried fruit, smaller plates piled with brown salt, jugs of wine and water, and stacks of flat bread. It is a feast both elegant and scrumptious, and a finer meal you have never seen, much less eaten.

This is a classic triclinium banquet, the great feast of a wealthy man (*are you getting hungry?*). You are eager to indulge in the festivities, but you wait in happy suspense for the host to assign you your seating position around the table. "Ah! I am to sit next to the host—a great honor!" And you proceed—slowly, so everyone can see—to make your way around the outside of the table to your esteemed seat at the feast. The magnificent triclinium is low, little more than a foot high, and it nearly fills the whole room. You carefully navigate the lumpy cushions lining the floor until you reach your assigned place, where to your delight you find there are plump pillows pressed snugly along the whole outside edge of the table. You have never before partaken of such elegance and comfort, and you want to do things properly.

But how do you actually dine at such a table? Chairs would be out of the question, because the people of that age living in that part of the world rarely used them for any occasion, if they ever even saw one. Besides, the table is much too short for chairs, and they would hardly fit in such a snug room. Tonight you will feast on the floor, and this is nothing new to you because you have eaten this way all your life. What *is* new to you are the cushions, for you have never lounged on anything so rich.

You happily plop down on the padding in front of your table setting, ready to begin the meal. But suddenly you notice that the other diners are not sitting at all—they are reclining. As they take their places around the table, all the other guests begin stretching out on the cushions, lying perpendicular to the edge of the table with their head toward the food and their feet to the wall. They are all leaning on their left arm, which means they are also lying on their left side, with their knees slightly bent and their bodies all facing the back of the person in front of them. Their feet, the dirtiest part of the body, are politely situated as far away from the food as possible. You imitate their position and find it enormously comfortable, though a bit awkward, because it is difficult to see anyone to your left—or is it behind you? But it does not matter, because it is *very* comfy and elegant. This is the *reclining position*.

Suddenly, your host, who is reclining on your right (or is it in front of you?), rises to a kneeling position. He takes a loaf of the thin, round bread from the table, and with both hands holds it up to heaven and gives thanks to God. "Amen!" he declares, and he tears off a small piece, dips it into a bowl of broth, reaches around to his left, and shoves it right into your mouth! The feast has now officially begun.

All the guests, reclining and leaning on their left arms, now eagerly begin reaching for the food with their right hands.

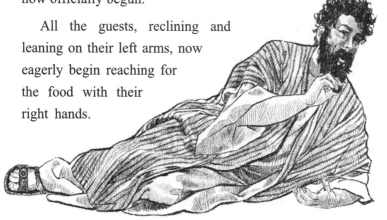

Some of the diners roll over onto both elbows to more easily view the rest of the table and chat with their neighbors, and you do likewise. As you look across the sumptuous table, there is movement everywhere, and you see the happy guests dipping bread and slices of meat into bowls of tasty potage. As they feast, they talk and laugh loudly, telling stories and catching up on the happenings in the wide world. Someone begins bellowing a familiar song, and everyone at the table joins in, erupting in laughter as it concludes. You recline again on your left arm, when all at once the man in front of you—your host and friend, leans back and plants his head squarely in the center of your chest. He tilts his head back, looks up at you and asks you about your journey and your family. You look down at his face and answer him, relating the adventures of the day and joyfully boasting about how your children have grown. Your friend laughs with delight, blesses you, and then rocks himself back onto his left arm.

The lively celebration fills the nighttime air with the sound of songs and merriment, lots of talk, and the clatter of clay pots and wooden bowls. But as the evening wears on, the festivities begin to slowly wind down. The oil lamps dim and begin to smoke and flicker out; and the guests yawn, rub their eyes, and grow quiet. But no one is leaving, because they do not have to; in fact, it would be foolish to try.

It is dark outside, pitch dark. How will you light your way home? There are no street lamps, and carrying a torch would mark you as a target for robbers who lurk in the night. So you do not leave the feast. And why should you? You are safe inside a fine house and the gates are shut and barred. Besides, you are reclining contentedly on cushions and pillows. Are you tired? No problem. No guestroom is needed, because you are welcome to fall asleep right there at the table. And when you awake in the morning, food and fresh drink is already on hand, and the festivities begin anew. In fact, if this were a wedding feast the celebration would continue for *seven full days*; if it were some other esteemed occasion the revelry might carry on for as long as two weeks! And if you were a poor peasant, such an event might be the happening of your lifetime. If ever you were invited to such a feast, you would never want to miss out.

Jesus was often invited to dine with people, some of whom were questionable, controversial, and even unsavory characters. But Jesus seemed willing to eat with whoever asked, and gladly.

Now, there was this one particular incident...

CHAPTER 11

"Do You See This Woman?"

In chapter seven of his Gospel, Luke describes a remarkable incident involving Jesus, a Pharisee named Simon, and a very sinful woman. A Pharisee was a demanding legalist, a teacher of the Law of Moses who felt that because of his great religiosity he towered above the peasantry. Pharisees also tended to be rich, and as a result they believed (and taught) that if you had wealth, then it was because God liked you (and they were quite convinced that God liked them *a lot*). Of course that meant that if you happened to be poor it was because God did *not* like you. But more than that, the Pharisees also piled oppressive burdens on the backs of the lowly, teaching them that to obtain God's favor they must carry out all their religious duties in the correct manner, which was, of course, exactly the way *they* did things.

It is no wonder that Jesus spent most of His ministry among the poor people of the land and had compassion for them. Neither is it a mystery as to why Jesus and the Pharisees constantly collided with each other. He would openly call them hypocrites, which meant "actors," because even though they were unquestionably devoted to God's law, they lacked any heartfelt affection for Him or His people. The Pharisees, in turn, would openly insult Him, disparage His "questionable" parentage, and make every attempt to publically humiliate Him. Originally fascinated by Jesus, their curiosity grew into a malicious envy because He began stealing their precious thunder, and the masses now followed Him.

One day the servant of a Pharisee named Simon approached Jesus, inviting Him to dine with his master at his villa. Although there were still a few Pharisees who kept an open mind about Jesus and fewer still who secretly admired Him, Simon was certainly not one of them. Jesus, of course, knew this about Simon, yet agreed to eat with him anyway. Jesus never seemed to turn down a meal with *anyone*.

So off Jesus went to Simon's house with the servant leading the way, and with them went all His disciples *and everyone else in the village*. This was a huge gathering of people who had invited themselves to this seemingly minor event, but they were not presuming on Simon's hospitality. In fact, Simon and Jesus both anticipated the presence of a large crowd at the dinner. There was an age-old custom in the land which declared that whenever two rabbis would meet together to discuss spiritual matters, everyone in the village was invited to come and listen. Such an event was part of their religious education tradition, for to hear two rabbis debate was considered a momentous, very public occasion.[*] And Simon was depending on it.

The villa would have been filling up with eager peasants as Jesus and Simon reclined at the table and commenced their dinner conversation. Though Luke did not record for us the nature of their discussion, it is possible that at least part of their dialogue involved the forgiveness of sinners. If Simon was a typical Pharisee, he would likely have asserted God's utter distaste for the disobedient, while Jesus would have declared His Father's great love for them. This is only a guess, of course, but such a discourse might account for what happened next…

As Jesus was talking with Simon He felt the sudden sensation of a warm bead of water dropping onto one of His feet, followed by another, and then another. The conversation abruptly halted as He turned to see what was happening. There at Jesus' feet stood a disreputable woman. Like a veiled shadow, she had quietly slipped into the room during the meal, somehow managing to press her way through the mass of people until she reached the place where Jesus was reclining. As she stood behind Him she wept; more than that, she sobbed, head in hands, her tears streaming through her fingers and dripping onto His feet. But these were not tears of sadness or pain, but of relief and release from some unbearable anguish. She wept for joy, and it was because of something He had said: something about God loving and forgiving wicked sinners—like her—and she believed Him.

---

[*] In modern Israel there is a humorous expression that suggests that whenever two rabbis meet together to talk you are guaranteed to have at least three opinions…!

Murmurs began to rumble through the crowd and some gasped, while others frowned and pointed. Every eye turned and glared at the woman, and stern faces leered at her with scorn and disgust. She was well-known in the village and she was vile, but their revulsion at her did not matter to her anymore; only HE mattered.

"My tears have fallen on His feet! Ah! I will wash them!" And crouching down behind Him she cradled the Master's dirty feet in her wet hands, showering them with a gentle rain of happy tears. Then slipping her hand up inside her head-scarf she let fall a long plait of dark hair (a very improper thing to do); and as she washed His feet with her tears she lovingly wiped them clean with her hair. And then she bowed down her naked head and she kissed them…

"But this is not enough!" she thought, "I must do more—He is worthy of so much more!" And fumbling inside the folds of her robe, she grasped a thin leather strap slung around her neck and pulled at it. At the end of the strap dangled an elegant alabaster jar, sealed with hard wax and full of very expensive perfume, a luxury so valuable that it may have been her entire dowry. She snapped open the seal and poured out the lavish ointment, drenching the feet of Jesus and overwhelming the stunned guests with the aroma of its pungent opulence. With her bare hands she tenderly massaged the rich perfume into His feet, still weeping and washing them, wiping and kissing them. She worshipped Him.

Simon the Pharisee, on the other hand, was disgusted with the whole scene. "If this man were a prophet," he scowled to himself, "He would know who is touching Him and what kind of woman she is—that she is a sinner." But Jesus knew what Simon was thinking, and He spoke up. Here is Luke's account of what happened next:

Jesus answered him, "Simon, I have something to tell you."

"Tell me, teacher," replied Simon.

So Jesus told him a parable:

"Two men owed money to a certain moneylender. One owed him five hundred denarii,* and the other fifty. Neither of them had the money to pay him back, so he canceled the debts of both. Now which of them will love him more?"

Simon replied, "I suppose the one who had the bigger debt canceled."

"You have judged correctly," Jesus said.

Then he turned toward the woman and said to Simon, "Do you see this woman? I came into your house. You did not give me any water for my feet, but she wet my feet with her tears and wiped them with her hair. You did not give me a kiss, but this woman, from the time I entered, has not stopped kissing my feet. You did not put oil on my head, but she has poured perfume on my feet. Therefore,

---

* A denarius was considered to be a day's wage.

I tell you, her many sins have been forgiven — for
she loved much. But he who has been forgiven little
loves little."

Did you notice? Simon was an outrageous host. At his
personal invitation he fetched Jesus to his villa, and then
brazenly refused Him hospitality: no water to wash His feet,
no welcoming kiss, and no anointing oil for His head. Even
more, his shocking neglect of his guest was likely intended
to broadcast a ruthless message to the masses: Jesus was
a contemptible man and not fit to be received by anyone.
Simon the Pharisee might have brought Jesus into his house,
but he would never welcome Him.

But did you also notice what the sinful woman did? She was
an outcast, a public and practicing reprobate. To Simon she
was repulsive, vile, and irredeemable; she was untouchable
except by the other foul reprobates of her ilk. For a rabbi to
even brush against such a degenerate was to be soiled by her
gross immorality. But the sinful woman sought Jesus, and
when she found Him she deliberately touched Him. More
than that, she worshipped Him, and Jesus, Himself a rabbi,
graciously received it. She took hold of Him and washed His
dirty feet when the self-righteous Pharisee refused Him the
courtesy; she kissed His feet with holy affection when Simon
would not bid Him welcome; she anointed and massaged
His feet with extravagant perfume, not the thrifty scented oil
withheld by the envious host.

The sinful woman lavished upon Jesus every gift of
hospitality at her disposal, not to welcome Him into a house,

for she, like Jesus, may have had no place of her own to lay her head. She lovingly received Him into the only place she truly owned, into the decaying ruin of a broken heart beating inside a ravaged body. And Jesus was delighted to receive such a splendid welcome into such an inglorious home; and He joyfully embraced the lost lamb who welcomed Him.

Then Jesus said to her, "Your sins are forgiven."

The other guests began to say among themselves, "Who is this who even forgives sins?"

Jesus said to the woman, "Your faith has saved you; go in peace."[21]

And she did.

There are few people in the Bible more strikingly dissimilar, yet at the same time more alike, than Simon the Pharisee and the sinful woman. Like Simon, many people have invited Jesus into their house, and you can tell. His picture, nicely framed and subtly lighted, is situated above their mantelpiece; His Book is proudly situated on the top shelf of a high bookcase along with the other great pillars of literature; and above the bedroom door hangs a small, reverent cross. And because He is in their house, they feel satisfied and secure, certain of God's approval because they have done these good things in honor of Him. But like religious Simon, they may have forgotten that they, too, are real sinners who are every bit as desperate for God's forgiveness as the wicked woman. This is what made them the same.

What made them different? The woman saw her sinfulness and hated it, while Simon's great religiousness blinded him to his own wretched condition, and he hated *her*.

Which are you? Are you more like Simon the Pharisee, or perhaps more like this woman? Do you believe you are a sinner in need of a Savior, or do you perhaps think that it is *others* who really need forgiveness? Either way, you now know where to find it. It's at the feet of Jesus.

> *The sacrifices of God are a broken spirit;*
> *a broken and contrite heart,*
> *O God, you will not despise.*

> – King David, Psalm 51:17–

> *Go in peace.*

CHAPTER 12

Clean Hands

Before we can eat my feast there is yet another tradition we must honor. You are about to touch my food and your hands are not clean to my satisfaction. I must wash them.

Of course, when you first approached my house a servant greeted you, clutching a small-spouted water pot and sporting a large linen towel wrapped around his waist. You were delighted to be met by him, and you eagerly extended your travel-wearied hands in his direction. He politely bowed his turbaned head and tilted the narrow spout downward, pouring into your open palms a refreshing flow of cool, clean water. Briskly rubbing your hands together and splashing the excess onto your face, you rinsed away the grime of the journey. Ah! Much better! And then you dried your hands and face on the servant's ready towel.

But you are my honored guest, and today I must make a special effort to see that your hands are

especially clean for my feast, so I will personally
wash them. And as I do I will also be reminding you
and the other guests of the salvation of God, and of
the Great Feast of the LORD. Truly!

Tradition! To the loveably distressed Tevya, the main character in the Broadway hit *Fiddler on the Roof*, tradition was the glue that held his Jewish world together. In the opening scene of the play, he proudly extols the virtues of a life governed by all sorts of staunch religious customs having to do with family roles, dietary regulations, relationships with Gentiles, and even the constant wearing of hats by men, a particular tradition about which he hadn't a clue. But it was still a tradition that must be observed because it had to have meant something important to someone once upon a time. So you just did it anyway, even if no one could remember why.

The Jews of ancient times were unusually fastidious and made it a rule—a tradition—to never touch food without first washing their hands. Few things in life, of course, are more basic and simple than washing your hands, but never underestimate what a religious legalist can do to the most uncomplicated of tasks.

For instance, shortly after He had returned from a brief stroll on the Sea of Galilee, some Pharisees and teachers of the law again approached Jesus. To these devout and determined legalists Jesus was the competition, which is why they had journeyed all the way from Jerusalem to scrutinize every detail of His ministry. They were trying hard to find a fault (or invent one) that they could use to demolish His enviable authority. And they thought they found one.

"Why do your disciples break the tradition of the elders?" they complained to Him. "They don't wash their hands before they eat!"[22] Their stern objection, of course, was intended as a public indictment, accusing Jesus of leading His disciples to carelessly neglect an esteemed local tradition, namely, that they did not wash their hands correctly.* Really. It was not even in the Bible, so the ritual possessed no authority other than the meddlesome weight they had placed on it, but it was the best they could come up with.

Their problem was this: when you washed your hands before eating a meal, you were to allow the water to first run down your hands and off the tips of your fingers, then raising your hands the water was to trickle down your forearms and off your elbows, then again from your fingertips, and so forth, seven times. To make matters worse, pots, pitchers and kettles required additional ceremonial washings before eating. Jesus and His disciples, however, probably only rinsed their hands once and in some ordinary fashion before eating their meal, thus offending the gang of snooty legalists.

Such traditions, of course, were burdensome and often tyrannical, especially if the poor practitioner has no idea why he must forever repeat a certain ritual, wear certain

---

* This incident may have occurred around the time of the Passover Feast, which would add weight to the accusation of the Pharisees.

garments, or say certain things in a certain way. But when you understand its original intention, a tradition can sometimes prove wonderfully enlightening. And in the time of Jesus it just so happened that a particular tradition about the way you washed your hands preached an amazing sermon.

If you were a guest of special honor at a feast, it would often be the proper duty of the host to personally wash your hands before you touched the food, even though you may have already refreshed yourself before entering the room. Now that you have taken your honored place at the table, I, your host, would set a bronze or copper basin on the floor before you. Being familiar with the custom, you would extend your hands out over the basin with your palms facing each other, perpendicular to the floor. I would then pour fresh water over your hands, thoroughly rinsing them, at which time you would do...*nothing*.

You would never rub your hands together or scrub. In fact helping is really not allowed, you just have to sit there and let me wash you. I would then grasp your dripping hands in mine and begin to cleanse them myself, scrubbing away the dust and grime of the day, rinsing and inspecting them to make sure they are completely clean to *my* satisfaction. After all, you will be eating at my table and touching my food. After looking them over front and back to make sure they are perfect, I gently dry them with a clean towel.

I now beckon for my servant to quickly remove the basin and dispose of its sullied contents, for I do not want you to dip your hands back into the dirty water. If you did, you would defile yourself all over again. Your hands are now thoroughly clean to *my* satisfaction, and you are finally ready to eat at my feast. And what did you do to help? *Nothing at all*, which is the whole point of this ancient tradition.

Do you see the lesson in all this?

King David, in his exquisite twenty-fourth Psalm, posed a very important question: "Who may ascend the hill of the Lord? Who may stand in His Holy Place?" In other words, who on this earth is good enough to stride into the throne room of heaven and boldly stand in the white-hot presence of God Almighty—and survive? What man could possibly gaze upon the glorious face of God without being reduced to a smoldering cinder, much less come away blessed and vindicated? David, of course, also gave us the answer: "He who has clean hands and a pure heart, who does not lift up his soul to an idol or swear by what is false."[23]

"Let's see," some will ponder, "I really want to go to heaven when I die, and I certainly want God to have a favorable impression of me when I show up. I'm certainly not an idol worshipper and I can't remember having ever sworn by Buddha or Zeus. I have always tried to live a good life so I think my heart is reasonably pure. But *clean hands*? Why do I need *clean hands* to be able to stand in God's holy presence? What does *that* mean?"

Think about it: what do we do with our hands? We *do things* with our hands; we work with them and provide for others with them. And if I have done only good things with my hands—if all my life I did good works that honored God and blessed others, then my hands are clean. But if I did bad works, if I ever treated others wickedly or dishonored God, then my hands are dirty. That's the metaphor, plain and simple.

Now, have you ever sinned? Then your hands are dirty in the sight of God—in fact the Bible plainly tells us that *all have sinned and fall short of the glory of God.*[24] So, David's two questions are staggering: who can ascend the hill of the Lord? Who can stand in His holy place?

I might reply, "Well, I have done pretty well but I certainly haven't lived a perfect life, so I suppose I don't have *perfectly* clean hands." Someone else may lament, "I have lived a terrible life, and my hands are stained and filthy!" But for both of us the problem is the same: how will we ever be able to enter the glorious presence of an absolutely holy God with dirty hands?

"Ah!" I think, "I know what to do! I must wash them, really hard and really clean—I will make up for all the filthiness of all my bad works with plenty of new clean ones!" And I begin scrubbing my own hands, rubbing and wringing them, polishing them to my own standard of moral spotlessness. But when I present myself before the Master of the Great Feast, will the cleanliness of my own efforts be enough to satisfy Him? He *is* perfect, you know!

This is the hope of so many people: that the scouring of their dirty old sins with new, clean works will be enough to completely wash away the dark stains of a lifetime of offenses and shortcomings, and that their noble efforts will somehow satisfy the flawless purity of God. But there is another, more pressing problem, namely, that our sins are like tattoos: they just don't wash off, no matter how hard you scrub them. So, who, then, *could ever* stand in His Holy Place?

Ah, but the Master of the Feast loves us! He has invited us to come and dine with Him at His own table, so He must be the One who will provide the means for us to come to the Feast with perfectly clean hands. How? *He* will be our hand-washer so that we can be made spotless to *His* satisfaction.

Now, look again at the hand-washing ceremony. You have been invited to the Master's House for the great feast, but you have dirty hands. But you are not worried. You are completely confident that you will recline at the magnificent Heavenly banquet, because you will not be the one washing your own hands—*He* will do it all. The Master comes to you and sets the empty basin in front of you. You happily extend your open, empty hands out over the basin and the Master drenches them with His pure water, that cleansing blood of His Son's perfect sacrifice for the sin of the world. And what do you do? *Nothing.* Then, with His own strong but gentle hands, the Master scrubs and massages from your soiled fingers all the filth and grime of the world, even cleaning the soot from under your fingernails and wiping away the deepest, most stubborn stains of life.

Without thinking, you start rubbing your hands as if to assist Him, but He gently reminds you that this is His job, and that you must stop trying to help. He rinses your hands and inspects them, and when He is fully satisfied He wipes them dry with a fresh towel. Then He takes the basin of dirty water, fouled with all your sins and failures, and He casts it out of His house, never to be seen or touched again. "I have washed your hands," He tells you, "and I have cast away all your sins. Now, be careful not to dip your hands back in the dirt anymore."

You are now clean to the Master's satisfaction. And what have you done to help? Nothing at all, except to simply let Him wash you. And *now* you are ready to eat at His Great Feast.

Are your hands dirty? All the scrubbing in the world—all the good works and best intentions—will never be able to wash away the dirty stain of our sins. But He can.

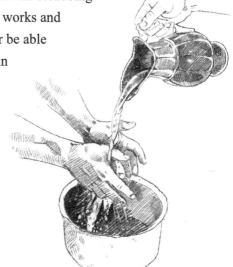

"Master," you cry out, "I want to come to your feast, but my hands are so dirty!"

"Stretch out your hands, my child," He replies, "and I will wash them clean for you."

This is how God's grace works.

"For it is by grace you are saved, through faith—and this not from yourselves, it is the gift of God—not by works, so that no one can boast."

– The Apostle Paul, Ephesians 2:8-9 –

CHAPTER 13

Bless the Lord

Your hands are clean, and so are your feet; your thirst is satisfied and your head has been perfumed and massaged. But before you or anyone else reclining around the table will touch the bountiful fare, we must first bless the One who has so generously provided for this grand occasion. You are so very grateful to your host for his tremendous kindness, but you and all the eager diners are keenly aware that were it not for the grace of another, more benevolent Provider, such a splendid event would never be possible...

As he was about to give thanks for a very special evening meal with our tour group, our Israeli guide declared, "In America when you pray over your meals, you bless the food. Here in Israel we bless the *Lord!*" Then, with his eyes wide open and looking up toward heaven, he held high in his hands a small pita loaf and prayed,

"Blessed art Thou, O Lord our God, King of the universe, who gives us bread from the earth."

Tearing the loaf in half, he broke off a bite-sized piece and ate it. Then he said, "Amen."

We were all amazed at his statement and delighted at his prayer, because we knew he was right.

Our guide was young, barely out of his twenties, but His prayer was ancient, of the Hebrews of old before the time of Moses. Yet to this very day the same prayer is still proclaimed by almost every practicing Jew. It is the "blessing" and "grace" of every meal, the giving of thanks to the Giver of all good things. It is a prayer whose subject and object is nothing so small as a fragment of food or as earthy as "the hands that prepared it," but the wonderful, gracious God of all goodness. *Blessed art Thou, O Lord our God, King of the universe.* And what might seem foreign and perhaps even a bit disagreeable to some of us Westerners is that Jesus would have repeated this same prayer daily...

Many American Christians practice a long established tradition, praying over a meal with heads bowed and eyes closed, and even with hands folded in reverent submission. In fact, when you see someone at the table pause to "bless the food," they might often assume this very familiar Christian pose. Those who pray out loud may even utter a poetic prayer that has been passed down from a long and rich denominational heritage. "For that which we are about to receive, may the Lord make us truly grateful," you might hear someone pray, or perhaps the delightful child-like declaration, "God is great, God is good, and we thank Him for our food."

Nowadays, however, you are more likely to hear a modern Evangelical Christian pray spontaneously over their meal, declaring "whatever the Lord lays on my heart" out of a concern that repeating the same prayer again and again might lack sincerity and truth. I have often heard people pray for God to "bless the food, that it might bring nourishment to our bodies," or to "bless the hands which prepared it." No matter which way we choose to pray, God loves to hear from His children and He delights in our gratitude; and sitting down at the supper table is an excellent reminder to thank Him for His loving provision. But when it came to mealtime prayers, the ancient Jews did things a little differently.

First, the Jews of that day would have prayed the exact same prayers at any ordinary meal, and, by the way, so would Jesus. Even though no such prayer is mentioned in the New Testament we must remember that Jesus was the ultimate Jew: He was everything His Father intended a Jewish person to be, and as such He would also have honored all reasonable Jewish traditions, including the way people commonly prayed. In fact, Jesus, in His magnificent teaching on prayer in the Sermon on the Mount, warned his disciples not against *repeating* prayers, but against "babbling like pagans [who] think they will be heard because of their many words."[25] And even though, according to the Bible, most of Jesus' prayers were spontaneous and from His heart, He would still have prayed the traditional prayers of the people—prayers that were so common and ordinary to the Gospel writers that they simply did not write them down. It may seem strange, even wrong, to modern Evangelical Christians to suggest that Jesus regularly prayed repetitive prayers. But remember: whenever Jesus prayed He always meant every word of it, because He never forgot Who He was talking to.

As they blessed the Lord, the ancient Jews also would not have bowed their heads, closed their eyes, or folded their hands. As Jesus was about to miraculously feed nearly twenty thousand people with five barley buns and two sardine-sized fish, Matthew tells us "He looked up towards heaven, He gave thanks, and broke the loaves."[26] At the conclusion of the Last Supper the apostle John observed that "[Jesus] looked toward heaven and prayed…"[27] Anyone could easily read right past these simple statements and never notice that they render an excellent sketch of how people did things thousands of years ago. Nowadays, of course, we bow and close our eyes (no peeking!) to foster an atmosphere of reverent intimacy with God. Jesus, however, reminded His disciples of that which they knew so well, that their Father was in heaven. This is why many Jews tend to look up when they pray.

But the ancient Jews did not stop at thanking God for providing bread. In fact, they would immediately follow the first prayer with a second, blessing Him for supplying their drink, namely wine.* They would set down their bread and take up their cup, lifting it towards heaven. Then they would proclaim,

"Blessed art Thou, O Lord our God, King of the universe, who creates the fruit of the vine."

Do you remember Jesus' first miracle? He and His disciples were invited to attend a wedding feast in the village of Cana, a lively event that would be celebrated for a full week. It was probably a few days into the feast when Mary, the mother of Jesus came to Him and announced, "They have no more wine." What happened next was not only miraculous, but an unexpected revelation of Jesus' true nature—one that would have been surprisingly obvious to any Jewish person reading John's account of the incident. How so? There was something about that little prayer they would say over the cup…

---

* For many Christians the drinking of wine is a contentious issue. For instance, some will ask, "Did the people of the Bible drink real fermented wine or just newly crushed grape-juice?" This age-old question has smoldered in the church for centuries, occasionally heating up guarded conversations, sometimes igniting fiery arguments. Of course attempting to declare an assured answer to such a feisty debate would be pouring gasoline on the coals. But if we look at the issue through the eyes and minds of the ancients, things sometimes make a little more sense. The Bible is chock-full of commands and condemnation against drunkenness of any sort, and except perhaps when administered as a painkiller to a dying person, even a slight "buzz" was considered a big sin. Then there is the strict ban against drunkenness in the Bible, which is a good indication of the potency of their wine, a feature for which "new" wine (unfermented grape juice) needed no warning. Further, when the Passover was celebrated, four cups of wine were to be consumed during the course of the festivities, which could pose an obvious problem. Traditionally, however, the Jews would dilute their Passover wine with three parts water to one part wine in order to avoid any unfortunate and irreverent incident.

When the wine was gone, Jesus' mother said to him, "They have no more wine."

"Dear woman, why do you involve me?" Jesus replied. "My time has not yet come."

His mother said to the servants, "Do whatever he tells you."*

Nearby stood six stone water jars, the kind used by the Jews for ceremonial washing, each holding from twenty to thirty gallons.

Jesus said to the servants, "Fill the jars with water"; so they filled them to the brim.

Then he told them, "Now draw some out and take it to the master of the banquet."

They did so, and the master of the banquet tasted the water that had been turned into wine. He did not realize where it had come from, though the servants who had drawn the water knew. Then he called the bridegroom aside and said, "Everyone brings out the choice wine first and then the cheaper wine after the guests have had too much to drink; but you have saved the best till now."

This, the first of his miraculous signs, Jesus performed at Cana in Galilee. He thus revealed his glory, and his disciples put their faith in him.[28]

Do you see it? His disciples did, and they witnessed His glory. And John, as he recorded the event, presumed that the

---

* Chronologically, these were Mary's last recorded words in the Bible, and never was wiser word spoken!

reader also grasped the grandeur of the moment. Think about it: at the beginning of the feast the host would have prayed over the cup, "Blessed art Thou, O Lord our God, King of the universe, *who creates the fruit of the vine…*" What is most amazing is that "O Lord, Our God, King of the universe" was there attending the wedding, enjoying the festivities, and when the wine ran out He answered the host's prayer *exactly*. The miracle of turning water into wine was a declaration in John's Gospel that Jesus of Nazareth was also God With Us, especially if you knew that little prayer. And now you know.

One more thing: even though the Jews of that day prayed the same prayers at every meal, they did indeed pray spontaneously—and they did so when it counted the most. Let me explain.

Have you ever sat down to dinner with a group of friends, perhaps at a coffee shop, when someone asks, "Who would like to say the blessing?" After a short and awkward silence, one of the more spiritual members of the party happily volunteers to render thanks. And you know what is about to occur. He begins to pray…and pray…and pray. The server, standing by with a dire look on her face and her arms laden with plates of hot food, waits uncomfortably to hear a closing "amen" that never seems to come (you know this because you peeked). Somewhat exasperated, she resolves to serve the dishes as unobtrusively as possible. As she slips your order in front of your bowed head, the marvelous aroma of your fresh hot meal fills your nostrils and tantalizes your eager taste buds. You are ready to plunge into your plate, but you are still praying—or at least the person at the end of the table is. "Amen!" he finally concludes, and you heartily agree. Now, you love to pray because you certainly love the Lord, but the fact is your dinner is now cold; and as you rue the woeful condition of your now flaccid order, the only thing you are chewing on is the regret that you did not do things more like the people of Jesus' day...

You already know how and what the ancient Jews prayed at the beginning of their meals. It was reverent, poetic, and brief, and once it was spoken the dining commenced. It was at the *conclusion* of the meal when someone would offer up to God a spontaneous prayer of thanksgiving for the food they had just enjoyed. And it made perfect sense. As you began, you blessed the Lord for giving you bread and creating wine, and later, when you were full and satisfied, you thanked Him in whatever manner gladdened your heart. Even better, you could pray as long as you liked without annoying hungry guests or busy servants.

There is a single example of this sort of spontaneous prayer mentioned in the Bible, but its occasion is positively spectacular. It is all twenty-six verses of John's Gospel, chapter seventeen. At the conclusion of the Last Supper, Jesus, knowing His arrest was at hand and that He would be nailed to a cross by morning, prayed what was quite possibly His most magnificent prayer. And this time it was not about the meal. He prayed for His disciples and He also prayed for those who would believe in Him through their message. And that means He also prayed for you: that you might be full of joy and protected from the devil; that you might be completely set apart to His purposes and be as one with each other as Jesus is with His Father; and that you might be with Him where He is. Now *that's* a prayer, especially in light of Who was actually praying. And the most amazing ingredient is *you* are in it. Here is what He said:

> *"Father, the time has come. Glorify your Son, that your Son may glorify you. For you granted him authority over all people that he might give eternal life to all those you have given him. Now this is eternal life: that they may know you, the only true God, and Jesus Christ, whom you have sent. I have brought you glory on earth by completing the work you gave me to do. And now, Father, glorify me in your presence with the glory I had with you before the world began.*

> *"I have revealed you to those whom you gave me out of the world. They were yours; you gave them to me and they have obeyed your word. Now they know that everything you have given me comes from you. For I gave them the words you gave me and they accepted them. They knew with certainty that I came from you, and they believed that you sent me. I pray for them. I am not praying for the world, but for those you have given me, for they are yours. All I have is yours, and all you have is mine. And glory has come to me through them. I will remain in the world no longer, but they are still*

*in the world, and I am coming to you. Holy Father,
protect them by the power of your name—the name
you gave me—so that they may be one as we are
one. While I was with them, I protected them and
kept them safe by that name you gave me. None has
been lost except the one doomed to destruction so
that Scripture would be fulfilled.*

*"I am coming to you now, but I say these things
while I am still in the world, so that they may have
the full measure of my joy within them. I have given
them your word and the world has hated them, for
they are not of the world any more than I am of the
world. My prayer is not that you take them out of
the world but that you protect them from the evil
one. They are not of the world, even as I am not of
it. Sanctify them by the truth; your word is truth. As
you sent me into the world, I have sent them into the
world. For them I sanctify myself, that they too may
be truly sanctified.*

*"My prayer is not for them alone. I pray also for
those who will believe in me through their message,
that all of them may be one, Father, just as you are
in me and I am in you. May they also be in us so
that the world may believe that you have sent me.
I have given them the glory that you gave me, that
they may be one as we are one: I in them and you in
me. May they be brought to complete unity to let the
world know that you sent me and have loved them
even as you have loved me.*

"Father, I want those you have given me to be with me where I am, and to see my glory, the glory you have given me because you loved me before the creation of the world.

"Righteous Father, though the world does not know you, I know you, and they know that you have sent me. I have made you known to them, and will continue to make you known in order that the love you have for me may be in them and that I myself may be in them."

–John 17–

Bless the Lord…!

CHAPTER 14

Bread of Life

"Bread is life, it is the essence of our being."

Journalist Haim Shapiro

I t took our breath away. It was late morning in the Old City of Jerusalem when our group, footsore from vigorous touring, halted awestruck under the vast canopy of its huge waning shadow. Towering over us loomed the colossal Western Wall of the Temple Mount.

Erected almost two decades before the birth of Jesus by King Herod the Great, "The Wall" was a massive barricade built of enormous limestone blocks set in place with such precision that a razor blade could not slip between them. Built to intimidate, it was the outer facade of a gigantic retaining wall that, two thousand years ago, surrounded the thirty-five acre platform that supported the magnificent Temple of the LORD.

Still imposing at a mere half of its original height, the twenty-four meter high "Wailing Wall" has, over time, become the most revered place in all the world for the Jewish people (being the spot nearest the holy sanctuary of their long destroyed Temple). It is a place of fervent prayer, brimming with bearded Jews clad in black and many devout women, all bowing and weaving and chanting as they face the mighty stones of The Wall. But it is also a place of exuberant celebration, a huge outdoor synagogue for lively bar and bat-mitzvahs, packed with revelers donning festive colors and men draped in blue-and-white prayer shawls.

It was a little before lunchtime on a clear, brisk January morning when our group paused near the base of The Wall. We could hear the murmur of many prayers and zesty conversations echoing across the Western Wall Plaza as our guide gathered us into a tight circle for instructions. "Go visit The Wall," he told us, "pray, talk to a Rabbi, take some pictures, and meet back here in fifteen minutes, where Pastor Jay is standing. After that, we will go get some lunch." I had just become home base. Our group quickly scattered, but within minutes a few people had returned, including two children who had accompanied their parents on the tour.

One of them was a lad of twelve years from the high desert of Southern California, whose name was Alan. Touring Jerusalem can overwhelm even the heartiest of visitors: trekking around the Old city is always physically demanding, and the Biblical sites (which are many) can be spiritually daunting—especially when the visitor is a child.

Alan was clearly overwhelmed, and, since the morning was late, he was getting hungry.

Kneeling down next to me, he unzipped the front pocket of his small daypack and pulled out a round, flat piece of bread that he had rescued from the hotel breakfast buffet for just such an occasion. Now, Jerusalem sits on a high ridge on the outer rim of a vast desert, and the air is very dry, which (unfortunately) the young man did not take into account. His bread was now stiff as a wooden plank. A look of deep disappointment pinched his face as he rose to his feet. But then he smiled. He had an idea…

Standing nearby was another young man from our group who appeared equally blasé about the morning's adventures. Alan, still smiling, motioned to the boy and said, "Hey! Go over there!" And the other young man ambled backwards until he was about thirty feet away. You can see where this is going. His voice echoed across the stony plaza as he shouted, "Catch!" and like a Frisbee, he flung the crusty pita in the direction of his friend. The other boy missed, and the bread fell clattering onto the limestone pavement. He quickly snatched it up and sent it spinning back to Alan, who also missed his catch. A game of bread Frisbee had begun right in front of the Western Wall—*the Wailing Wall*—the holiest place in all the world for the Jewish people. Oy.

To everyone's shock, our guide went ballistic. In an instant, he seized the stale disk and said (none too quietly), "What are you doing? Don't you know that's *bread*?" Alan and his young friend stood as if thunderstruck. "You *never* mistreat bread in Israel!" rebuked the guide, "You treat it with respect here! Do you understand?" The boys nodded sheepishly, still unable to grasp the gravity of the situation. But they also never did it again. "I will dispose of this properly, later," the guide told me, and he slipped the loaf into his own weathered daypack.

Later that day, I discovered that our guide had pulled the bread from his pack and laid it on a small shelf protruding from a stone wall somewhere in the Old City. It was a place where hungry people could find leftover scraps to eat. In Jerusalem you would *never* treat as rubbish something as precious as *bread*.

To the Jewish people, bread is more than mere food; it is life, it is the essence of their being,[29] and it has remained that way for thousands of years. As it is for many Jews today, the ancients respected and reverenced bread—so much so that it was considered evil to cut it with a knife. In fact, to demonstrate your gratitude to God for blessing you with the bounty of the earth you broke it, tearing the loaf in half. If you offered a piece of bread to a friend you presented it to them gently, holding it with both hands, as if you were giving them that which was life to them.[30] To the Jew bread is life. But where did they get such a notion about this simple, basic piece of food?

It is not hard to imagine that if you didn't have any bread you would starve, which is why throughout the ages bread has well represented life. This makes perfect sense, of course, because for much of the world bread has always been its most essential food, and when it is gone life is soon to follow. But for the Jews, God wanted bread to mean so much more to them than food. And it all goes back to the familiar story of the Passover...

Unchained from nearly four hundred years of miserable slavery by the mighty hand of God, the Hebrews were at last set free from the brutal bondage of Egypt. Within hours of their departure, backs to the Red Sea, Pharaoh's pitiless army attacked their huge defenseless camp, bent on their annihilation. But you know the story: God parted the sea, allowing the Children of Israel to escape on dry ground, fleeing between the looming walls of upright water. He destroyed Pharaoh's army, crushing them under the terrible weight of the sea as it collapsed down upon their deadly pursuit. And with free eyes gazing back across the churning expanse toward the land of their bondage, this enormous mass of hopeful, often doubtful people soon discovered that they had an entirely new problem.

They were now perched on the fringe of a vast and relentless wilderness that they needed to cross: a realm of scorpions, sand, and scrubby little bushes. What is more, the sheer number their huge wandering host may have exceeded two million people.* Now, what are they going to eat?

You probably know this next part of the story as well. God solved their desperate problem by giving them *manna,* a nutritious, honey-sweet substance that formed each day like

---

* Exodus 12:37 tells us that more than 600,000 men "on foot" or literally of "fighting age" left Egypt that day, a number which did not include the women, children, old men, or the "other people" who went up with them.

dew on the ground, except on the Sabbath. *Manna*, which meant "what is it?" was simply miraculous. It was God's marvelous provision, the "bread from heaven" as it became known, and it kept the Children of Israel alive throughout their longer-than-expected journey to the Promised Land. Simply put, God gave it, the Hebrews ate it, and they lived. The bread was from heaven, it gave them life, and they were to remember it every time they ate. So, whenever the Jews broke bread, the loaf was meant to remind them that even though many died there in the wilderness, it was God who gave them life. And that is why they reverence bread.

But God always seems to have deeper, more profound intentions for His great acts in the Bible. He wants to say something and He wants people to listen, and manna says something. It was a signpost that pointed to His Messiah, who, like bread, would come from heaven. He would be the One who would give life to all who "ate" Him as they wandered in the wilderness of this world. It was as if to say, "Whenever you hold bread, I want you to remember that it was I who kept your forefathers alive with My miraculous bread. But that bread was only a shadow of how I will one day provide you with life—*eternal* life. Remember this, because when I send you the true Bread from Heaven, if you take Him and eat Him, this time you will live forever." And then Jesus came, and He explained it to us…

The day after He had fed thousands of people with the five barley loaves and two dried fish, Jesus was teaching under the shady colonnades of the Capernaum synagogue.

Once again He found Himself thronged by hundreds of eager followers. But the masses which sought Him that day were not interested in what He had to say to them as much as they were in another free lunch. It also happened to be right before the Passover Feast, so this is what He told them...

Jesus said to them, "I tell you the truth, it is not Moses who has given you the bread from heaven, but it is my Father who gives you the true bread from heaven. For the bread of God is he who comes down from heaven and gives life to the world."[31]

"I am the bread of life. Your forefathers ate manna in the desert, yet they died. But here is the bread that comes down from heaven, which a man may eat and not die. I am the living bread that came down from heaven. If a man eats of this bread, he will live forever. This bread is My flesh, which I will give for the life of the world."[32]

That day the people did not like what they heard. In fact, they were out-and-out offended, so much so that from that time on *many of His disciples turned back and no longer followed Him.*[33]

Can you picture Jesus standing in the packed synagogue, pointing to Himself speaking these startling words amidst a growing din of grumbles and gasps? You might have been offended, too. *He* is the bread of life? *He* is the manna from heaven, and whoever eats that bread will live forever? *He* is what God had in mind when long ago He gave the Children of Israel the miraculous manna?

It is an electrifying image, especially for the Jewish people who have continually reverenced their bread, but have long forgotten why. You can read the complete account of this provocative incident in John's Gospel, chapter six.

This, too, you will need to remember later on...

CHAPTER 15

Mind Your Manners

P lease, thank you, you're welcome, would you please pass the peas, don't talk with food in your mouth, keep your elbows off the table, don't slurp your soup." Sound familiar? These are but a small taste of the countless table manners we learn (well, most of us) from the moment we can hold a spoon. Politeness, of course, is part and parcel of our everyday lives, especially if we want to get along with each other (much less render due respect to a fellow human being).

But when people dined together in the days of Jesus, politeness would have looked quite different from the common courtesies with which we are so familiar. If we watched Jesus eat a meal with His disciples, we would probably find it difficult to contain our bewilderment (and perhaps even our laughter) at some of the things they would do. But the ancients were dead serious about their meal customs because they knew that neglecting a single table manner could badly insult your host or upset the other guests. Let me tell you about five of them.

The "Right" Hand

Do you remember how you would have reclined at the supper table? You lounged on your left side, which meant you had to lean on your left arm. This would also mean that that arm was immobilized, forcing you to eat only with your right hand, which was the whole idea. Why? You never touched food with your left hand, *ever*. Let me explain.

There is a very old reason for this custom, one that reaches way back, far beyond the times of the Bible. It is also the same reason that many people in today's world will only touch food with their right hands. Your right hand was considered the *kosher* hand, the *clean* hand, so you would use it especially for "clean" duties, such as touching food or greeting friends. But what about your *left* hand? This is a rather delicate matter, but simply put, during the ages before the invention of toilet paper, people would use their left hand exclusively to tend to their daily hygienic needs. Needless to say, even washed, you would never touch food with your unkosher hand, because everyone knew what you did with it.* In fact, if you were at a meal and you touched (even accidently) a morsel of food with your left hand, the host would have the item removed from the table, because you just defiled it. By the way, this

* This table manner applied to all food at the table except the bread and baked eggs. Two hands were needed to break bread, thus the right-hand-only custom was overruled by a very practical need. Concerning baked eggs (baked because the ancients would not have wasted precious water boiling them), since you were not going to eat the shell, a person could hold the unshelled egg in their left hand while peeling and eating it with their right.

is why we shake right hands when we greet, and why some Middle Eastern cultures punish thieves by cutting off their right hands. Now you know.

One Sabbath day, as He was teaching in the Capernaum synagogue, Jesus noticed a man in the crowd who had a withered right hand. The Bible does not tell us how it happened, but the man had been afflicted long enough for the musculature of his lower right arm to have badly atrophied. Jesus, who always seemed drawn to the people with the greatest need, said to the man, "Get up and stand in front of everyone." It also happened that a band of handwringing Pharisees had slipped in to scrutinize His every move, hoping He would do something they could use against Him. Luke tells us what happened next:

> Then Jesus said to them, "I ask you, which is lawful on the Sabbath: to do good or to do evil, to save life or to destroy it?" He looked around at them all, and then said to the man, "Stretch out your hand." He did so, and his hand was completely restored.[34]

Do you see it? That day Jesus did far more than heal a man's paralyzed hand. He healed his *right* hand, which meant *He also restored the man to fellowship with others*. He made him kosher, He made him *clean*. Until that wondrous moment no one would eat with the man because he was only able to touch food with his left hand, and in those days if you ate alone there was something terribly wrong with you.

Jesus heals, and not just our bodies; He restores our broken relationships and brings us together with each other and with His Father. He makes us *kosher*. Even more, the Bible tells us that Jesus is now seated at His Father's *right hand* interceding for us. And one day, when He comes again as King, He will gather at His *right hand* His sheep, to whom He will say,

> *"Come, you who are blessed by my Father; take your inheritance, the kingdom prepared for you since the creation of the world. For I was hungry and you gave me something to eat, I was thirsty and you gave me something to drink, I was a stranger and you invited me in, I needed clothes and you clothed me, I was sick and you looked after me, I was in prison and you came to visit me."*

> *Then the righteous will answer Him, "When did we see you hungry and feed you, or thirsty and give you something to drink? When did we see you a stranger and invite you in or needing clothes and clothe you? When did we see you sick or in prison and go to visit you?"*

> *The King will reply, "I tell you the truth, whatever you did for the least of these brothers of mine, you did it for Me."*[35]

They are at His right hand, the most *kosher* place in all the universe, and they are clean because of Him. They are rewarded for the goodness they have brought into the lives of others, because to care for others is to care for Him. They are the sheep of His hand, His *right* hand, and His Father will bless them.

Another king, David, said,

You will show me the path of life; In Your presence is fullness of joy; At Your right hand are pleasures forevermore.[36]

What a place to be! In fact, the writers of the Psalms likened God's right hand to that which teaches and upholds, gives refuge and is mighty to save; it is filled with righteousness and does valiantly, and it delivers and searches out enemies. Solomon learned that long life is found in the right hand of understanding. For Isaac, Jacob, Ephraim, and Jesus Himself, the son of the right hand received the double portion of the family inheritance. And if all this was not enough, after He ascended to His Father, Jesus sat down at the right hand of the Majesty in heaven.

The *right hand* meant so much more to the people of Jesus' day, for in their minds there was no mightier, more holy thing than the right hand of God. Perhaps it will now mean more to us as well.

"You Do Me Honor"

"Would you please pass the hummus?" someone asks you. On the table next to your cup rests a clay bowl of the creamy garbanzo dip, just out of reach of the person dining next to you. "Certainly," you politely reply. Then, cradling the bowl and passing it to your eager neighbor, you say to them, "You do me honor." Of course, they expected to hear you

utter those words, because it is always an honor for
one person to serve another...

Today, if you and I were eating a meal together and you asked me to pass an item of food to you, I would say something like, "No problem—here it is," and hand you the plate. All is well: you have your food and I can now get back to eating my supper. Two thousand years ago, however, if you asked me to pass you something on the table, you were asking me to become your servant. "You do me honor," I say to you as I pass you the item. "I am happy to be your servant," I am telling you, "and it honors me that you would ask me to serve someone as worthy as you." Do you remember the gesture at the greeting? As I touched my forehead it was as if to say, "With my thoughts I worship you—I esteem you as greater than myself." Here it is again.

Life nowadays is too often all about *me*, and the people of Jesus' day seemed to understand just how unfulfilling and (dare I say it?) ungodly such an attitude could be. Many stores and companies will advertise, "You're Number One!" or "It's All About You!" Even some prominent Christian authors have appealed to our *me*-ness with titles about how *you* can be a better *you*, and so forth. But "me first" does not work well at all, especially in God's economy. To be "number one" I must struggle my way to the front of the line (wherever it might be), and when I finally get there I have to work hard to stay there. And when I eventually lose my place to someone else (which I will), I have to work harder, perhaps climbing over others as I go, to get back to my spot, a place that I am certain to lose again. This is not only true in business, it is true of life itself; and that means it is also true of *me*.

Think about it: who are our most enduring heroes? I am not referring to our trendy icons who are admired for their sports abilities or dashing good looks, or even to those who have very publically achieved their great human potential (whatever that is). They are one-minute wonders who are soon forgotten. *Enduring* heroes, however, are much different. They are remembered.

But what was it that carved their memory so deep into timeless stone long after they had passed from the scene? They were rarely stylish, nor were they typically admired for their athletic or musical abilities, and they tended to have unremarkable faces. But they are remembered: Harriet Tubman, David Livingstone, Hudson Taylor, Florence Nightingale, Raoul Wallenberg, Corrie Ten Boom, Janusz Korczak, Albert Schweitzer, Mother Theresa, Annie Sullivan, Martin Luther King, Jr., Irena Sendler, and the like. Why do we remember them? It was not because of their *self*-esteem. They are just a few of the mostly nameless people who heard the frail cries of the world's forgotten, pleading, "there is something I need but it is out of my reach." They are the ones who said with their lives, "You do me honor." They were happy to be your servant. And that is why their names endure.

So, it is not only an honor "to be your servant," it is also *wise*. And supper is a perfect place to remind us each day that the greatest in the Kingdom of Heaven really is the servant of all.

Bread and Honor

You have been reclining comfortably at the fabulous table, anxious to partake of the sumptuous fare, when the host suddenly straightens himself into a sitting position. As you watch, he reaches for a loaf of bread, gives thanks, and then tears it into two uneven pieces. The other diners turn in rapt anticipation to watch what the host is about to do. Taking one of the halves, he breaks off a small, bite-sized piece and with his right hand he dips it into a bowl of warm broth resting on the table in front of him. Lightly shaking the loose drops off the wet bread, the host raises the morsel, reaches around and slips it into the mouth of the person to his immediate left. The other guests nod and murmur with approval.

At first glance, this table manner is just strange. In fact, in my travels teaching about Biblical feasts to all kinds of people in many different countries, the reaction to this table custom has been nearly identical everywhere I have taught. *Laughter*. To the people living in the days of Jesus, however, it was a very different story.

If someone at your table tore off a small piece of their bread, dabbed it into their dipping bowl, and then stuffed it into your mouth, they were sending you a clear and colorful message. With everyone watching they were saying to you, "You are my brother and I would gladly lay down my life for you. You are my friend. I honor you, I esteem you, and I love you." And at times, it even meant, "I forgive you." This was not only a powerful and affectionate declaration of brotherly love, it was also one of the greatest honors a person could bestow on anyone...

The average third-world prison bears little resemblance to the extravagant gray-bar Hiltons of the United States. The often-brutal conditions compel inmates to compete for food, drugs, and their very existence. Internal security is lax, guards are often corrupt, and vicious fights and murders are commonplace. It was in one such facility in Latin America where, following a Biblical Dinner with eighty inmates, I witnessed a truly amazing thing. Amidst the noisy crowd milling around in the stuffy cement chapel I noticed two men, each slipping a piece of bread in the other's mouth and hugging. I had seen people do this before, of course: tearful friends honoring one another with bread after a Biblical Dinner, having been deeply moved by the whole experience. Needless to say, I paid little attention to them and busied myself with the cleanup of the room. Later that same evening, while standing in the doorway of his humble church, the pastor who had arranged the prison visit pulled me aside.

"Pas-tor Jay," he said in broken English, "I tell you something good," and he smiled. Now speaking through our interpreter, he asked me, "This morning after the Biblical Dinner, did you see those two men with the bread?"

"I think so," I replied, "Are you speaking of the men who were hugging?"

"Yes. Pastor Jay, you need to know that they are both murderers who were sworn to kill each other, and that today they made peace. They ate bread together. They are brothers now."

"You are my brother and I would gladly lay down my life for you. You are my friend and I honor you, I esteem you, and I love you. I forgive you."

Imagine being able to say all that just by putting a piece of broken bread in the mouth of a friend—or an enemy.

***

It was still more than an hour before breakfast. I was foraging for an early snack in the hospitality lodge of a retreat center where hundreds of men had gathered for a conference. "Bananas? Nope—I'm allergic. Cookies! Ah, well, not before breakfast—my mother taught me better than that. Let's see, ah! Bagels! A bagel will do nicely." I snatched up a shiny brown wheel of bread, broke it, and began nibbling away as I ducked out the door, heading off to the morning assembly. With my red daypack slung over my shoulder and a chunk of bagel in my hand, I munched my way across the broad plaza in front of the grand meeting hall. There, amidst the flood of men pouring into the building, I noticed a sturdy, graying man with thick glasses. I recognized him instantly.

He was a long lost friend, and it had been several years since we had spoken, the last time being his bitter confession to a devastating sin. Striding quickly towards him our eyes met, and his lips pursed in sudden regret. I could see the hesitation in his body as he clasped his hands in front of him and rocked back slightly on his heels. Now standing face to face, he extended his hand in a guarded offering of peace, a doubtful look in his eyes.

"What is this?" I thought. "He never shakes hands. This man only gives crushing bear-hugs." All in the wink of an eye, I broke off a small bite of bagel, reached out as if to shake his hand, and instead thrust the bread into his mouth. He had once been to a Biblical Dinner, and he suddenly grasped what had just happened. It took a few moments for me to recover from the hug.

"You are my brother and I would gladly lay down my life for you. You are my friend. I honor you, I esteem you, and I love you. And I forgive you."

This brings to mind another incident having to do with Jesus and the happenings at a particular Biblical feast. But we will get to that later…

Thank You for Serving Me

Everything is just right: the food is hot and plentiful, the servants are busy, and your companions are kind and sociable. As you are thoroughly enjoying your meal you notice your neighbor reach for a baked egg, peel it, and sprinkle it with brownish salt. As he begins to raise it to his mouth you casually reach over, seize the egg from his hand, and eat it. "Thank you! That was delicious," you tell him, and he smiles graciously and begins peeling another egg.

Truly. Now, to most Westerners, this odd table manner would be fun, perhaps a silly game of skill and stealth, and by all means a hilarious one. A couple of thousand years ago, however, it served simply to remind the people, especially at suppertime, that they were all one big family who lived close-knit lives. In fact, this odd custom kept them in the habit of serving each other without complaint, reminding them that it was a far greater blessing to live for the good of others than for one's own self. It also helped to keep things a little more light-hearted in a world where life was hard and dangerously unpredictable: that there are always others we can depend on—and who can depend on us—to help.

"It is more blessed to give than to receive,"[37] Jesus told His disciples. This saying is not a command, but a proverb, a spiritual truism along the lines of "a man reaps what he sows."[38] In other words, it is not about obeying a command, but living life the way God designed it to be lived. It is about *others*, and when we place others before ourselves, even when they are a bit "grabby," God's approval will rest upon us, and that means *blessings*. And this is not just a cheerful sentiment that pops up once a year around the glowing hearth-fires of Christmastime, it is everyday life the way Jesus meant it to be.

A fascinating tale is told of General William Booth, the founder of the Salvation Army. The account might be legendary, but it is also wonderfully provocative. The story goes that around 1900 the General was preparing to send his annual Christmas greeting to all his Salvationists serving around the world. Since this had to be done by telegraph, which charged for each word sent, the whole process proved quite expensive. Times were tough that year, and it was calculated that there would only be enough money available to wire a single word to each missionary. The one-word message the General chose to send simply said, "Others!"

Gayle Erwin, author of the book, The Jesus Style, put it like this: the true test of whether or not you have a servant's heart is in what you do when someone treats you like one. For the ancient Jews, this table manner tested that idea every day.

Just the Once, Please...

Ancient meals were dipping meals, and the people of that day were good at it, mainly because they followed one very strict rule: they never, never, never, never, never, never, never double-dipped. They were that fastidious.

I just thought you would like to know.

Chapter 16

Jerusalem

I hope you are enjoying the festivities! The revelry will continue for many days, and there will be more singing and laughing, story-telling and dancing, and, being a humble peasant, more food than you have ever seen. The delicious aromas of roasted meat and fresh-baked bread linger in the air, mingled with the tangy scents of cooked leeks and incense. Gluttony is strictly forbidden, of course, so there is plenty of time to take walks with friends and catch up on the news of the wide world. It is a fine feast and a glad respite from a hard and tedious life.

But now it is time to visit yet another feast, one immersed in a blend of ancient ceremony and prophetic fulfillment. It is nighttime in Jerusalem, the moon is bright and full, and the echoes of chanting and singing fill the cool spring evening. The distant moan of a Temple shofar* resonates across the Cheese-maker's Valley, drifting into the glowing window of a kataluma in the quiet southwest corner of the City. Inside the second-story guest room, pale plastered walls flicker in

---

* A ram's horn trumpet

the warm dance of burning torchlight. There is a triclinium in the center of the room, carefully set with all the ceremonial foods required for a traditional Passover feast. The table and its rich settings are all ablaze with yellow light, illuminated by thirteen olive oil lamps, one for each of the men reclining around its outer edge. They are eager for the feast to commence, for this is a very special evening for all Jewish people. It is Passover.

But three of the men are unusually quiet on this most festive of occasions. One seems distant, as if he is far away, lost in deep thought, and his demeanor is bittersweet. The second is oddly evasive in his conversation and unwilling to look his friends straight in the eye. The third is just plain irritated.

One of the diners at the table glances up at a star-lit window as he hears the lonely sigh of the shofar.

"It is time to begin," he says, and looks intently at the Host.

Welcome to The Last Supper...

PART FOUR

The Last Supper
(Revisited)

CHAPTER 17

Dinner Reservations

J esus' disciples tended to argue. A lot. In fact, the longer they walked with Jesus the more they seemed to bicker, and it was almost always about the same thing. Two of the disciples even plotted against the other ten, hoping to manipulate Jesus into settling the argument in their favor. Their little coup d'état backfired, of course.

I often picture Jesus strolling along a rocky path and talking about the Kingdom of God with an eager crowd of local peasants, His disciples in tow. Suddenly His happy conversation is soured by a spate of angry words erupting a short distance behind. "Oy," the peasants hear Him sigh as he buries His face in His hands, "Here we go again…"

What was their problem? The Bible tells us that they were squabbling about who was the greatest among them. Of course the whole thing sounds so petty, and in reality it was—but not to them. Were they arguing about which one of them Jesus liked best, as if being considered the closest friend of the greatest living rabbi made them a celebrity? Perhaps their clash was more political in nature: that if Jesus was to be King, then "the greatest" might be the one He would appoint as His prime minister or to some other prominent post. But what was the real issue that raised the hair on the back of their necks and provoked such outbursts of petty niggling? Simply put: *dinner reservations*.

The disciples, dense as they often were, understood a few things that are easily overlooked by modern eyes. First, they suspected that Jesus was the Messiah, the "Anointed One" who was sent from heaven to establish God's perfect kingdom on the earth. They also seemed to know what Isaiah the Prophet wrote about the Messiah's kingdom, that it would begin with a great feast.[39] And they knew that according to table etiquette, the most important guests—the greatest at the feast—sat at the immediate right and left hands of the host, which would have been Jesus. But most of all, the disciples knew that *there was a pecking order around a triclinium table*, an order of importance based on where you sat, and they constantly knocked heads over which of them would be chosen to dine closest to the Messiah on the day that He established His kingdom. This was why they argued.

Whenever you attended a feast, everyone would know how important (or unimportant) you really were by where you sat. At a wedding feast or when eating a meal at home, people usually reclined around the table according to their age, the oldest dining in the most honorable spots, the youngest at the far end. At a special occasion such as a kingly feast or a Passover celebration, the seating order was often quite different. Remember the "U" shape of a triclinium table? If you were to view it from above with the opening of the "U" at the bottom, the most honorable positions would be located along the left side of the table. These people were important, so they sat in the best seats. Those who reclined along the top edge of the "U", even though they occupied the central position of the table, may or may not have been of any particular renown. But the people who sat along the right wing of the table were looked upon as the lowest, the least, and the last. *Nobody* wanted to sit there.

One spring afternoon, as He and his disciples were ascending the long, steep road from Jericho to Jerusalem, the mother of James and John, Mrs. Zebedee, approached Jesus and knelt down in front of Him. Matthew the Apostle tells us what happened next:

"What is it you want?" He asked.

She said, "Grant that one of these two sons of mine may sit at your right and the other at your left in your kingdom."

"You don't know what you are asking," Jesus said to them. "Can you drink the cup I am going to drink?"

"We can," they answered.

Jesus said to them, "You will indeed drink from my cup, but to sit at my right or left is not for me to grant. These places belong to those for whom they have been prepared by my Father."

> *When the ten heard about this, they were indignant with the two brothers.*[40]

Indignant is a rather diplomatic word, considering the circumstances. They were *furious*. Why? James and John were brazenly trying to manipulate Jesus into offering them the two best seats at the Great Feast of the Messiah, which they all believed was at hand. What made matters worse was their shameless exploitation of their own mother in their attempt to influence Him. "After all," they must have reasoned, "even Jesus could not say no to a good Jewish mother!" But perhaps the most irritating thing of all was that the other disciples did not think of it first. James and John were scheming to lock in their dinner reservations at the Messiah's feast.

Another time, when Jesus was invited to eat at the house of a prominent Pharisee, He noticed the other guests scrambling for the most honorable seats at the table. Jesus, of course, could not remain silent in the face of such silly self-importance. So He spoke up and told them all a parable…

> *When someone invites you to a wedding feast, do not take the place of honor, for a person more distinguished than you may have been invited. If so, the host who invited both of you will come and say to you, 'Give this man your seat.' Then, humiliated, you will have to take the least important place. But when you are invited, take the lowest place, so that when your host comes, he will say to you, 'Friend, move up to a better place.' Then you will be honored in the presence of all your fellow guests.*

For everyone who exalts himself will be humbled,
and he who humbles himself will be exalted.[41]

Can you picture the lesson? People often yearn to be celebrated and strive to be first. This partly explains America's obsession with celebrities—those colorful folks who are famous for being famous. But the economy of the kingdom of heaven could not be more *different*. If you want to exalt yourself then watch out. The Master of the feast is unflinchingly honest, and He knows you and knows where you really belong, and in front of all the other guests He will see to it that you sit there. But if you humble yourself and take the last seat, the lowest seat, the Master will come to you and tell you where He thinks you *really* belong, and escort you there personally.

"He who humbles himself will be exalted." Why? Because the one who humbles himself shows he has an honest appraisal of who he really is *on the inside*, that he has no real reason to be proud, and that he loves the truth. The Master likes that.

Let's go back to the incident with James and John on the road to Jerusalem. They wanted to be the greatest and they wanted to be first, so they conspired to make sure no one doubted their lofty status by arranging to sit next to Jesus at the left wing of the table. But Jesus had something else to say about their pithy plot:

"Can you drink the cup I am going to drink?" He asked them.

"We can," they answered.

"Are you willing to suffer like Me in order to be great?" This was the question He was asking James and John. "Yes, we are!" came their pompous response. But as Jesus pointed out to them, they did not know what they were asking. So He gathered His irate disciples and explained it to them…

Jesus called them together and said, "You know that the rulers of the Gentiles lord it over them, and their high officials exercise authority over them. Not so with you. Instead, whoever wants to become great among you must be your servant, and whoever wants to be first must be your slave—just as the Son of Man did not come to be served, but to serve, and to give his life as a ransom for many."[42]

Do you see it? Let's say I pulled a lottery ticket out of my pocket and said to you, "Here, this is the winning ticket—it is worth millions of dollars and I will *give* it to you. There is just one catch: you are going to have to suffer before I hand it over to you." A few people would probably storm off grousing, "No way! It's not worth it!" But if you are like me, before walking away from such a fortune you would probably ask, "What is it that you want me to do?"

You see, many people are willing to suffer much to gain certain things, as long as it benefits them in the end. In fact, every day we can see people putting themselves through all sorts of grief to become rich, famous, or powerful. But have you noticed that it is the ones who have suffered for the benefit of *others* who are the most admired people of all? They are the people for whom the world's great monuments are built: men who stormed the bloody beaches of Normandy, or who signed a Declaration of Independence that would also become their death warrant.

But they are also the ones whose monuments are held only in the heart of God: an abandoned mom working three jobs to feed and clothe her little ones; a Down-syndrome teen stirring a big pot of boiling soup in an inner-city homeless shelter; an exhausted relief-worker cradling a starving orphan in an African refugee camp. They are the kind of people who are truly the *greatest*. They are the ones who are most like Jesus, who suffered more than anyone to be the servant, literally, the *slave* of others. Many would endure much for fame, fortune and clout, but how many would deliberately suffer to become the slave of all?

It is from among such as these whom the Father will choose to sit at the right and left hands of Jesus at the Great Feast. This is the economy of the Kingdom of God.

By the way, one of the brothers got his wish...

CHAPTER 18

Table Talk

S o there was a pecking order around a feast table. The disciples understood this, of course, and they busied themselves plotting to sort out their dinner reservations, jockeying for the very best seats.

Now, if the Last Supper table was indeed a triclinium (which it most likely was), and the disciples held to the customs and manners of such a meal (which they appear to have done), then we can determine *from the Gospel accounts* where four of the men actually sat at the great feast.

But the real surprises emerge when we find out *who* ended up sitting *where*, and *why*...

Jesus: The Host of the Feast

If we were to believe Leonardo da Vinci's famous rendering of the Last Supper, Jesus would have been seated at the exact center chair of a long, elegant table, flanked on both sides by His anxious apostles. And like the arrangement in da Vinci's painting, we, too, would probably expect to find the most important person at a great banquet situated at the middle seat of a similar type of table, surrounded (hopefully) by happier people. But things were radically different at a triclinium feast, and for good reason.

To His disciples Jesus was the Rabbi and the Master, and though some of them still had their doubts, most believed He was also the Messiah.[43] He was also the one who made the arrangements for the feast and sent Peter and John to take care of the details.[44] At the meal He prayed for the bread and the cup.[45] All of this points to Jesus as the host of the feast.

At this point we need to go back to our angel's-eye view of the table, that upside-down "U" shape with the opening of the "U" at the bottom. From this angle the V.I.P.'s would be sitting on the *left*, which meant that the host would have reclined somewhere along that edge of the table. This is where it helps to know a little something about their customs. Traditionally, the host always sat at the second seat from the end on the left wing of the table, with the two most honorable guests seated on either side of him. This means that the most important places at the feast were the first three seats along the left side of the table, with the host in the number two position.

Why this peculiar arrangement? It grew out of a fearful necessity, one that especially concerned the honorable fellow reclining in front of the host, at the host's right hand...

The Bodyguard

It is nighttime, and you have just clambered up an uneven flight of steep wooden stairs leading to a small balcony and a low doorway. You grasp a rickety handle and push, and the door creaks open, groaning slightly on its worn, leather hinges. You take a step inside the room; it is stuffy yet dazzling in its subtle lamp-lit splendor. The flickering clay lamps are set neatly on the worn wooden surface of a grand triclinium table, its "U" yawning open toward the creaking door—toward you. The table is large and full of food, and there are thirteen men reclining snugly around its outer edge. Naturally, they all turn and look at you, to see who is interrupting their Passover meal. Because they are all resting on their left elbows, the men to your right are also facing away from the door and must painfully crane their necks up and over their left shoulders to give you a glance. The men reclining across the back of the table cock their heads slightly and with less difficulty as they look up at you. But the three men on the left are looking straight at you. Reclining on their left arms, their whole bodies are facing the door and you, as if in readiness to react to some imminent threat, and none more than the man at the near left-end of the table. He is glaring straight at you and his right hand reaching for something long and shiny on the bare floor in front of him. A sword! All at once you notice his body tensing up, as if he is about to spring to his feet in defense of those reclining behind him. "Wrong room!" you quickly apologize, and hurriedly duck out of the kataluma, hastily latching the noisy door behind you. Scurrying down the steep stairs you leap over the bottom three steps, land hard, and vanish into the night...

Of course, as far as we know no one interrupted the actual Last Supper, but if you had, this is the sort of scene into which you might have stumbled. But who was this edgy character at the left end of the table, the man who was reclining in front of the host? And why did he have a sword?

The answer is as simple as it is practical. The man to the host's immediate right was the one person in the room who reclined between the host and the door. He was known by many titles: the *best friend of the host*, the host's *right hand*, the *doorkeeper*, and the *wine taster*, and tradition demanded that he fulfill each of these honorable duties vigilantly. He was the *bodyguard*.

Those were dangerous days, and if you had an enemy they would not just sit around and say bad things about you. For thousands of years, people in that part of the world felt they had the right to exact public revenge for any harm someone may have caused them or their family. Now, the host of a feast was usually an important person, and important people tend to collect enemies. A feast was usually a very public event, which meant that just about everyone knew where the host was going to be during a certain span of time—including anyone who might hate him. This is why the host traditionally had a bodyguard reclining next to him, right in front of him, between him and the door.

To be the bodyguard of the host was an extremely honorable position at the table: the host trusted this man with his life, and the man loved the host enough to gladly lay down his life to protect him from all harm. He tasted the wine before the host drank it, in case it was poisoned. And if an enemy was to burst through the door and threaten the host, all the bodyguard had to do was lay back, falling on top of him and shielding him with his entire body. And just in case he needed it, he always had a sword resting in front of him. *Best friend, right hand, door keeper, wine-taster, bodyguard.*

John.

John? How do we know that? The answer is quite simple: *he told us.* John was the apostle who wrote down the most detailed account of the goings-on at the Last Supper. At one point during the feast Jesus stunned His disciples when He announced that one of them there at the table was going to betray Him. John, in his Gospel, tells us what happened next:

His disciples stared at one another, at a loss to know which of them He meant. One of them, the disciple whom Jesus loved [John], was reclining next to him. Simon Peter motioned to this disciple and said, "Ask him which one he means." Leaning back against Jesus, he asked him, "Lord, who is it?"[46]

John tells us here that it was he who was reclining next to Jesus, in front of Him, at His right hand. He got his wish. But there is something else: John, at the end of his Gospel, reminds us that he was the disciple "who leaned back against Jesus at the Supper."[47] The King James Version of the Bible says that he "leaned on His breast at supper." What an odd thing to mention! Or was it?

Think about it: if you were John and you were reclining on your left side in front of Jesus, you would be facing the door and Jesus would be behind you (in the same bent position), facing your back. So how would you talk to each other? Would you just flop over onto your right side to face Him, disheveling the mats and cushions, knocking against the table, and making a mess? Actually, all you would need to do to speak with Jesus is lean back. Your head would land in the center of His chest, you would look up at His face, and He would look down at yours. The conversation is on. *The disciple who leaned on Jesus' chest…*

As a dyed-in-the-wool American, if you and I were to have a conversation, I would feel quite comfortable standing across from you at a slightly bent-arm's length. Not too close and not too distant, just right for both of us. Personal space in the Middle East, however, has always been much closer. In fact, in my many conversations with Arabs and Turks, they have often stood so close to me that it felt as though they had to smell me in order to speak with me. This is quite awkward to your average American (to say the least), but in it there is also a healthy physical closeness that expresses friendship and acceptance with righteous intimacy; and it certainly speaks volumes more than a comfortable amount of space. It can be seen when two Jews greet with a holy kiss or when two Arab men hold hands simply because they are friends.

It is this same cultural closeness that also allowed grown men reclining around a low table to casually lay their head on their neighbor's chest so they could talk. By the way, were you to do the same as John, I think you would find that you could also hear the beat of the Master's heart.

The Guest of Honor

"I tell you the truth, one of you will betray me—one who is eating with me."[48] Jesus' startling words resonated with scandal and sadness. "Treachery!" reeled the stunned disciples, "How is that possible? Which of us is He talking about?" And His offended followers erupted into a chorus of grief mixed with an uncharacteristic contriteness: "Surely not I?" they cried.

Unable to contain his rabid curiosity, Peter, who was reclining at the opposite end of the table, managed to catch John's eye with a sharp nod. "Ask Him which one He means," Peter croaked in a raspy whisper meant only for John's ears. John agreed and leaned his head back on Jesus' chest. "Lord, who is it?" he asked. Looking down at John's upturned face, Jesus answered, "It is the one to whom I will give this piece of bread when I have dipped it in the dish." Then, straightening Himself into a sitting position, He broke off a small piece of bread, dipped it into the bowl in front of Him, reached around to His left, and slipped it into the mouth of the *Guest of Honor*.[49]

It was Judas Iscariot.

And at the very moment the bite of bread entered Judas' mouth two amazing things happened...

First, John tells us in his Gospel that the moment Judas received the bread Satan entered him. This is an astonishing observation, because in light of all the accounts of demon possession mentioned in the Bible, this one stands alone. The dark thing that entered Judas that night was no demonic underling, but the Evil One himself. The spiritual battle that raged on that pivotal evening just escalated to an entirely new level of warfare.

People have speculated for centuries about Judas Iscariot's motives for betraying Jesus that night. Strangely, much of the talk tends to excuse him as a poor, misguided patriot who, with the best of intentions, was only trying to force Jesus to take up the sword, destroy the Romans, and establish God's kingdom on earth. Sadly, (the theory goes) Judas' plan crumbled before his eyes as he watched his friend and Master led off to be crucified, prompting his tragic suicide. Thus, he became just another misunderstood martyr for the cause of freedom.

But the Bible does not say this. It tells us that Judas was a thief, stealing from the community moneybag, which the disciples had entrusted to him. Even more telling were Jesus' words as He prayed for His disciples at the conclusion of the

Supper. "None has been lost," He said to His Father, "except *the one doomed to destruction...*"[50] Jesus was speaking here about Judas. In the King James Bible version of this prayer He calls him *the son of perdition*. There is only one other person in the Bible ever referred to by that fearsome title: *the Antichrist.*[51] Judas was not some tragic patriot. In fact, he was a villain of the first order.

This brings us to the second amazing thing. The instant that Jesus put the bread into Judas' mouth, the disciples believed then and there *that Judas could not possibly be the betrayer*. Huh? Absolutely. Listen to what John said about that moment:

> *"What you are about to do, do quickly," Jesus told him, but no one at the meal understood why Jesus said this to him. Since Judas had charge of the money, some thought Jesus was telling him to buy what was needed for the Feast, or to give something to the poor. As soon as Judas had taken the bread, he went out. And it was night.*[52]

Jesus clearly marked Judas as the betrayer, but the disciples refused to believe it. Why? First, Judas was apparently the most trusted man among the disciples. He was the keeper of the moneybag, and they would not have deliberately given the bank to some shifty-eyed, hand-wringing thief.* Judas was also the guest of honor, which meant that Jesus personally selected him to sit in that enviable seat.

---

* Judas, it was later discovered, was indeed a thief and had been dipping into the bag for his own purposes (John 12:6)

But there was another, more compelling reason why they could not believe he was the betrayer: you would *never* put bread into the mouth of your enemy. You might bust him in the nose or grab him by the seat of his tunic and toss him out the door, but to honor your enemy with bread in front of everyone? It would never have entered their wildest dreams. But it should have.

Three years before that fateful night those same twelve disciples listened as Jesus taught the masses on the rocky slopes of a Galilean hillside. His message that day was both radical and controversial, and it upset their moral apple cart with many hard and shocking sayings. One of these sayings cut a bit deeper than the rest: "You have heard that it was said, 'Love your neighbor and hate your enemy.' But I tell you: Love your enemies and pray for those who persecute you, that you may be sons of your Father in heaven."[53] Not long after, Jesus repeated His stunning message when He reminded them, "But I tell you who hear me: Love your enemies, do good to those who hate you, bless those who curse you, pray for those who mistreat you."[54]

It seems they did not hear too well that day, or perhaps they did not wish to. If they had, they would have understood that Judas was indeed the betrayer by what Jesus did with the little piece of dipped bread. And they also would have understood how much He loved him, even to the very end.

You are my brother, Judas, and I would gladly lay down my life for you. In fact, tomorrow I will. You are my friend, though I do not seem to be yours. I honor you and esteem you, though I hate what you do. I love you. And I forgive you.

This is how to treat an enemy.

How do *we* treat our enemies? We all seem to have them, but the question is what do we do about them? The answer, if we listen to Jesus, is one of the great revolutionary distinctives that mark our Christian lives. Anyone can be kind to a friend: "Do not even pagans do that?" Jesus asked.[55] What sets us Christians apart in this world is the way we treat people who *hate* us, *curse* us, and *harm* us. Love them, He told us. But just how do we do that?

"Well, I love 'em in the Lord," many have proudly declared, but rarely has an emptier phrase passed through Christian lips. To love our enemy is not some warm, gooey sentiment that God slathers on us so we can feel cheery about a scoundrel bent on our destruction. In fact, it is not a feeling at all. Let me explain.

"Love" is a very peculiar word in the English language: I can love pizza, cats, friends, sunsets, golf, jazz, knitting, a good book, and (especially) God. Of course, such sentiment has less to do with love than it does with us merely liking the things that make us happy. In other words, we love the things we feel good about. But what about our enemies? Jesus definitely commanded us to love them, and we certainly do not feel good about them.

But the love He spoke of was not the same elastic word that we tend to casually toss around in our everyday conversations. When Jesus commanded us to *love* our enemies the word He used was the Greek expression, *agapé*, which, in the Bible, is considered the highest form of love. It is not the love of brothers and sisters, nor is it in any way sexual; it is not romantic or like the rewarding love of a warm friendship. What, then, is left? Much indeed.

Agapé can love vile villains and petty persecutors, and it can also love traitors. It is God's love for us, it was Jesus' love for Judas, and it is also to be our love for our enemies. This sounds impossible, and it would be—if *agapé* was merely a feeling. Many people pray for God to bless them with a great love for the people who hate them. But what they are really praying for is a lovely feeling of heavenly affection for their enemy, much like the supernatural fondness they believe God had for them before they were saved. But that is not how it works.

Agapé is more of an action than it is a feeling. *Agapé* is a love that is determined to do good, to bless, and to pray for people you may not even like. *Agapé* is a choice. Think about it: God loved us, *agapéd* us, even while we were still His *enemies*.[56] But did He feel *good* about us as we went about rebelling against Him and doing evil? It would not seem so, since the Apostle Paul reminds us that we were once objects of His wrath. In fact, He did not have to like us at all, but (and this is very good news) while we were still sinners, Christ died for us.[57] He did not *feel* good about us anymore than a loving father *feels* good about a rebellious and wicked son, but the father still does that which is loving and good for that son anyway. It is a love that leaves feelings of affection far behind in the dust; it is a love that takes action and does for others, even the worst of others, that which is good and right for them in the eyes of God.

That is *agape*. And when Jesus put bread in Judas' mouth marking him as the betrayer, He was demonstrating in full view of His oblivious disciples that which He had gone through many great lengths to teach them: He loved His enemy, even to the bitter end.

And that is how we are to love our enemies.

One last thought: if John was the disciple who leaned on Jesus' chest, then on whose chest did Jesus lean...?

The Last Man

Peter. Just the mention of his name by a Gospel writer usually meant that something painfully embarrassing was about to happen. Peter was impulsive, brash, bull-headed, curious, loyal to a fault, surprisingly tenderhearted, and he frequently opened his mouth only to change feet. He liked to be first, and he was the kind of man who would tell you that he *should* be first. But at the Last Supper, Peter appears to be reclining at the last seat on the extreme right wing of the table. This would mean that he was not only dining at the humblest part of the table, but that he was also occupying the worst seat in the house. At the Lord's great supper Peter was last—*dead last*. And it appears that he did not like sitting there—*not one bit*.

But how do we know that it was Peter who was reclining in this disreputable spot? Our first clue is found in his ability to catch John's eye. Do you remember when Peter, boiling over with curiosity, signaled John to ask Jesus who the betrayer was? John would have been reclining at the left end of the table facing the door. From that position he could see few, if any, of the other disciples, except for the man opposite him at the extreme right end of the table. Since John could see him, Peter appears to have been in that dubious seat.

Now, there are several ideas about how Peter may have ended up sitting in the worst seat in the house (why was it the worst? *We will get to that in a moment, too...*). Since he was assigned to help prepare the feast, it is possible that Peter was involved in some last-minute arrangement when the other disciples piled into the room and took their places at the table. Of course, no one would ever want to sit in that last position, so when Peter went to take his place there was only one seat left. We can only imagine the grumbling and growling that might have followed.

A second possibility is that Peter sat down in the lowest place on purpose, mainly because he wanted everyone to see how truly *humble* he was. Then, when Jesus noticed him *humbly* sitting there in that lowest of places, He would surely say to him, "O, Peter! You are *sooo humble*! Move up higher, here, by Me..." But if this was Peter's tact, Jesus never did play his game.

Another likely scenario is that Jesus told him to sit there. We can almost hear Peter's pained plea at that fateful decision,

"Why, Master? Please, don't I deserve better on this night? Am I not your Rock?" But whatever the reason Peter ended up in the worst seat in the house, Jesus never moved him. In fact, it appears that Peter disliked having to sit there so much that he launched into a tacit little protest, as you will see.

But what was so wrong about that place at the table? Why does it appear that Peter resented sitting there, and why is any of this even important? The answers are told in something that Jesus did that night, something startling and magnificent. In fact, what He did revealed to His disciples (and to *us*) what the Apostle John hailed as *the full extent of His love*. And that sounds like a *lot*.

It was still quite early in the evening when Jesus unexpectedly arose from the meal. Stepping over John, He ambled His way to the far end of the table, where, there on the floor He found a clay jug full of cool water, a broad basin, and a sizeable linen towel, clean, dry, and neatly folded. The disciples may have murmured and shifted uneasily as they watched Jesus quietly strip Himself down to His loincloth, wrap the large towel around His waist, and lift the basin and the pitcher off the wooden floor. Then He turned and looked down at John.

"What is He doing?" some may have whispered. "I don't know! Why is *He* doing *that*?" another might have hissed. And as the murmurs mounted, Jesus slipped between John and the plastered wall, knelt down, and began to wash John's feet. His *dirty* feet. Bewildered, John may have shot an unhappy glance across the table at Peter and then turned again to watch the Lord, the Rabbi, the Master tenderly scrub the dust from his filthy feet with cold water and bare hands. Without a word, Jesus mopped John's feet with the large linen towel that had now become His new tunic. Judas was the next man reclining at the table, and He washed his feet, too. And then the next, and the next, and on around the great table until, as John told us, He came to Peter. And Peter spoke up.

"Lord, are you going to wash my feet?"

Jesus replied, "You do not realize what I am doing, but later you will understand."

"No," said Peter, "You shall never wash my feet."[58]

What was Peter's problem? It is time for us to add things up: Peter was reclining in the last seat, which is the worst in the house. He did not want to sit there (nor did anyone else), and he lodged his protest by refusing to perform the unpleasant duty traditionally assigned to the man sitting in that lowest of seats. And what was that?

Wash Feet.

The pitcher, the basin, and the towel were conveniently arranged on the floor right in front of the last man, just in case there was no other servant on hand to perform the ugly task. If there was no one else, *he* automatically became the footwasher. So it was on that night that the job fell to Peter. The problem, however, was that everyone's feet were still dirty. And we can almost hear his bristling thoughts: "I'm no footwasher—I shouldn't even be sitting here! I'm better than this and everyone knows it! Let someone else do it!" And someone else did, but to his astonished horror, it was the last person he expected, and now that man was crouching down behind him, intent on washing his feet.

"No, you shall never wash my feet."

Peter's pious words here are often characterized as the almost angelic pleadings of an unworthy child. "Oh, I'm just not *worthy*, Lord. You shouldn't do *that* to little ol' me." Ah, so *humble*. But that is more in tune with the Hollywood version of the story. It is far more likely that Peter's tone was one of grief and pained regret, and for good reason: almost certainly he, more than anyone else at the table, knew who this foot-washing man was.

Six months before that momentous night, while they were travelling through the remote northern finger of Israel, Jesus called his disciples together and posed to them a curious question. "Who do people say that I am?" He asked them. They had heard a lot of speculation, of course, so they told Him, "Some say you are John the Baptist, others say you are Elijah or Jeremiah, or one of the other prophets." Then Jesus asked them another question, perhaps the greatest of all questions, though they may not have known it at the time: "What about *you*? Who do *you* say that I am?" And Peter stepped forward…

Simon Peter answered, "You are the Christ, the Son of the living God."

Jesus replied, "Blessed are you, Simon son of

Jonah, for this was not revealed to you by man, but by my Father in heaven…"[59]

From the moment he received that grand revelation, simple Peter seemed to understand that Jesus was not *just* a rabbi, the Master, the leader of their little movement. He was a man, yet so much more than any man who ever lived; He was the One who had come to them out of an everlasting past, the very embodiment of everything God ever told of Himself. He was the singularity of human existence, the confluence where all of God and all of man flowed together as one; He was the Messiah, the Anointed One whose coming was foretold from ancient times, the Son of the Living God, God wrapped in human skin, God *with* Us. And now Peter, reclining defiantly in his lowly spot, watched helplessly as the Lord, the Redeemer of Israel, the Savior of world, God in human flesh, the greatest in the Kingdom of Heaven, willingly and lovingly performed the worst job in the world, *Peter's job*, the one Peter thought he was too good to do.

His thoughts reeled in the unsolvable mystery of the man now kneeling at his dirty feet. To let *Him* wash his feet would be a monstrous travesty.

"No," said Peter, "you shall never wash my feet."

But Jesus' gentle insistence on washing his feet was never meant to shame him; it was simply the Royal hospitality of the Kingdom of God. Footwashing, remember, was a gift and a *welcoming*.

Jesus answered, "Unless I wash you, you have no part with Me."

"Then, Lord," Simon Peter replied, "not just my feet, but my hands and my head as well!"[60]

Peter really loved Jesus, and you can tell by his delirious reaction to his Master's persistence: "Then give me a bath!" he cried, "I want you, Lord, with all my heart!"

It was then that Jesus did a most extraordinary thing, something that would have made the angels gasp. He did not brusquely wash his feet and then thrust the equipment back at Peter saying, "There. You see? I did your job for you. Do better next time, Peter." Instead, He knelt down behind that last man, the lowest man, and ever so gently washed the dirt off his feet. And at that moment, Jesus—the Messiah, the Redeemer of the world, God With Us—became the footwasher *of a footwasher*.

Do you see it? This was the full extent of His love: Jesus, Maker of the universe clothed in human skin, humbled Himself, bowed beneath the lowest of the low, and washed a footwasher's feet—even one who was so defiant and proud. By morning He would be nailed to a Roman cross, condemned as a criminal and executed in the most ghastly of ways. It was there, on the bruised shoulders of His bashed and bleeding body that He would carry off the just penalty for the sins and wickedness of every person who ever lived, is living now, and ever would live. And having done so, even the worst sinner—the lowest of the world's low—could now be washed clean of their unholy filth. Penalty paid, once for all. On that cross Jesus washed *all* our feet so that there is no one so low or so bad that cannot be saved. The Apostle Paul put it like this:

Who, being in very nature God, did not consider equality with God something to be grasped, but made himself nothing, taking the very nature of a servant, being made in human likeness.

And being found in appearance as a man, he humbled himself and became obedient to death — even death on a cross!

Therefore God exalted him to the highest place and gave him the name that is above every name, that at the name of Jesus every knee should bow, in heaven and on earth and under the earth, and every tongue confess that Jesus Christ is Lord, to the glory of God the Father.[61]

***

After Jesus finished washing Peter's feet, He unwrapped the damp towel from around His waist, slipped back into His tunic and resumed His place at the table.

"Do you understand what I have done for you?" he asked them.

"You call me 'Teacher' and 'Lord,' and rightly so, for that is what I am. Now that I, your Lord and Teacher, have washed your feet, you also should wash one another's feet. I have set you an example

that you should do as I have done for you. I tell you
the truth, no servant is greater than his master, nor
is a messenger greater than the one who sent him.
Now that you know these things, you will be blessed
if you do them."[62]

"I have set an example for you…" This was the only time in the Bible when Jesus said these words, and it was about washing another's feet. But how do you do that? It might be possible to sneak up behind some unwary parishioner after church, tackle them, snatch the shoes from their feet, and start scrubbing away. Some churches offer special "foot-washing" services in order to practice this humble example (though it is not wise to announce such an event lest the people show up with really clean feet).

But perhaps washing another person's feet means a little bit more than a pail of water and a bar of Lava soap. Perhaps it is sitting down next to someone who is not so nice or so clean as we are used to and saying to them, "Would you like to talk? I would like to listen." Maybe it is noticing one of those invisible people, a wallflower or a social reject, and going over to pray with them or invite them to a meal. Or maybe it is sitting silently, holding the hand of a grieving mother or a destitute father. These are but a few of perhaps a billion other ways of washing someone's feet. All it takes is the humble courage to strip off our airs, take hold of the utensils that no one else is willing to touch, and kneel at the dirty feet of another human being, even if it is a stubborn one.

There is one more thing about Peter and the place where he sat at the table, and it is perhaps the most important thing of all. Just a few days before, you may remember, Jesus gathered His disciples together to speak to them, partly to keep them from coming to blows over the incident with Mrs. Zebedee and the pompous request of her sons James and John. You may also remember that it was there that He told them,

> *"You know that the rulers of the Gentiles lord it over them, and their high officials exercise authority over them. Not so with you. Instead, whoever wants to become great among you must be your servant, and whoever wants to be first must be your slave— just as the Son of Man did not come to be served, but to serve, and to give his life as a ransom for many."*[63]

This is the final piece of the puzzle. That night at the table Jesus went from the *greatest* to the *least* to the *greatest*. He stepped away from His dignified position as host and became a footwasher to His men. As God measures greatness, Jesus' willing humility also assured that He was the greatest in the Kingdom of Heaven and the most blessed man in the room. But He also did Peter's job because Peter refused to do it. That wretched seat was a curse to him, a post for worthless slaves. Peter wanted to move up higher, to a place of glory and adulation. But, if you think about it, he did not have to. Though he did not see it at the time, *Peter was already sitting in the best seat in the house.*

And that night he missed one of his greatest opportunities.

But later he would understand...

Which seat do *you* sit in?

Which seat do you *want* to sit in?

Don't miss out, because, as Jesus promised, *"Now that you know these things, you will be blessed if you do them..."*

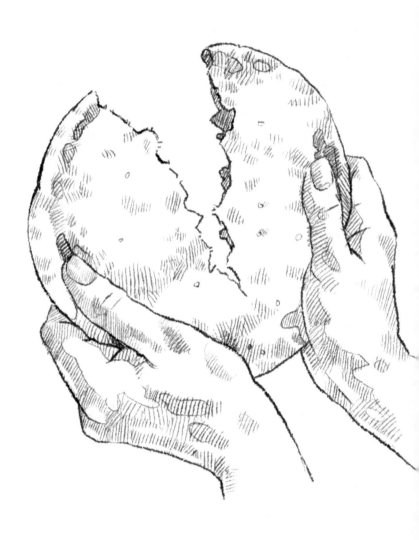

PART FIVE

Broken Bread

CHAPTER 19

One

Y ou have quarreled with your friend. It was over
something petty and foolish and nobody meant for
it to happen, but now you are at fierce odds with
each other. Even so, you both deeply regret the whole incident
because you really do love each other. But now you both
must do something to make matters right. Married couples
will "kiss and make up," and friends will shake hands or hug
and "let bygones be bygones." But some offenses, even the
little ones, are hard to forget, and many creep back in like
the tide.

For thousands of years, however, Middle-Easterners have
practiced a flavorful custom that was meant to permanently
reconcile enemies of all sorts. It arose out of a completely
different way of thinking about relationships, and its message
was so simple and wise that it was nothing short of inspired.
When two people found themselves at odds with each other
they would sit down and eat a meal together. They would
break bread.

Here is how they thought about this: Let's say you and I had a serious quarrel. After the dust has settled and the adrenaline has receded, we both realize that we ought to reconcile with each other. We arrange for a small meal and sit down together to eat. At some point during this meal, I would take a single piece of traditional flat bread and tear it in half.

Now, this is important: having done this I am *not* holding *two* pieces of bread in my hands—I am still holding *one* piece of bread that is now in *two parts*. I then give to you one half of the *one* piece of bread, and you eat it, and I take the other half of the *same piece of bread* and I eat it. The bread goes into your body and becomes part of you, and the same piece of bread goes into my body and becomes part of me. Now we are related to each other, because we have both eaten the *same* piece of bread. The bread has made us *one*.

Still confused? Think of it this way: that which has just become part of you has also become part of me. That makes us kin under the skin, as it were, and the broken link of our damaged relationship has now been re-forged in bread, which is mightier than iron. And whatever the reason for our quarrel, it is now permanently set aside by both of us and never revisited again. We have been *reconciled*.

But there is more, and it lifts our thinking about bread to a whole different level. Suppose there were two kings who were at war with each other. Their kingdoms were ravaged and ransacked from a long and bloody conflict, and their people wounded and frightened. One day one of the kings opened his eyes and saw the desolation of his subjects and

Broken Bread | 155

wept. It was they who were paying the terrible price for his pride and crown, and the king repented. "I will confess my wrongs in this war and I will send word of it to my enemy," he thought. "I will ask him if he will meet with me so that we may bring peace to the land." So the sorrowful king sent a messenger to his enemy, inviting him to come and dine in peace with his master.

If the other king agreed, both rulers would arrange to come together for a great feast in a safe setting, perhaps a no-man's land on the border between their two realms. As they arrived, their stately entourages would prepare a great feast-table of fine food and drink, and they would set up two royal thrones facing each other. As the two kings arranged themselves on the thrones the festivities would commence, their nobles dining uneasily across from each other, anxiously awaiting one especially important moment.

Finally, the remorseful king calls to a servant to bring him a loaf of bread. Receiving it, he tears it in two and hands one of the halves to his adversary. This was the great moment of hope and triumph anticipated by all the suspenseful diners at the feast, a breathless drama that would unleash a vast sigh of relief for all the inhabitants of the two devastated lands. Their kings ate bread together.

Now there would be peace between those two kingdoms for as long as the two kings live. They are now brothers; they are now *one*. It was called a peace-meal.

Bread is a remarkable thing...

Mightier than the Pen

It was an unusually quiet October afternoon in Israel. The day was relaxed and solemn, synagogues were packed with worshippers and the streets were nearly empty of the usual torrent of noisy little taxicabs. It was Yom Kippur, the highest holy day for the Jewish people, and it was 1973. A little after two o'clock in the afternoon, the quiet ended.

On that sleepy Jewish holiday the leaders of Egypt and Syria, bent on the obliteration of the modern state of Israel, launched a joint surprise attack. After one week of fighting, Israel, her soldiers desperate and exhausted and their equipment dangerously depleted, teetered on the brink of annihilation. But as they entered into the second week of fighting the tide of the war began to shift, and miraculously: the imminent downfall of Israel rapidly turned into a crushing rout of their attackers. By the end of the week the Israeli Defense Forces had fought to within sight of both Damascus and Cairo before they halted. Egypt and Syria were broken and humiliated, but they also remained unrepentant.

In the four years following the notorious invasion Egypt and Israel had hardly fired a shot at each other, but the two nations remained at a de facto state of war. Then an amazing thing happened. In November of 1977 during a mostly lackluster television interview, Egyptian President Anwar Sadat stunned CBS News reporter Walter Cronkite by announcing his intention to go to Jerusalem and begin peace talks with the Israelis. Cronkite hastily arranged the phone calls between Cairo and Jerusalem, and the next day Israeli

Prime Minister Menachem Begin officially invited Sadat to visit Israel. In less than a week he would be the first Egyptian leader to enter Jerusalem's gates seeking peace—ever.

A month later Prime Minister Begin and President Sadat met again, this time in Egypt, where their talks were not nearly as warm as they had been in Jerusalem. It was all downhill after that, and in the following months all hope for any sort of peace rapidly eroded. It was then that United States President Jimmy Carter, who was desperate for a successful peace process, stepped into the widening gap and did perhaps the wisest thing of his career: he invited Begin and Sadat to the presidential retreat at Camp David, Maryland in the hope of achieving a lasting peace between the two foes. For twelve grueling days the sequestered leaders conferred and clashed until they finally hammered out what has come to be known as The Camp David Accords. There would be peace.

Six months later Carter, Begin, and Sadat sat down together at a stately wooden table in front of the White House, before a festive throng of several hundred reporters and dignitaries. As the world watched in guarded anticipation, the three men put pen to paper and signed the great document. Then, laying down their pens they arose from their chairs, broke into broad smiles, and took each other's hands, shaking them vigorously. The world cheered and hailed the men as peace-makers, calling loudly for a Nobel Prize. Then everyone went home: photographers hustling off to their darkrooms and reporters to the ready keys of their idle typewriters. To the Western world the process was complete and everyone was now content. They had stopped watching—and they missed the most important part of all.

A few weeks later Begin and Sadat met once again, this time in the southern Israeli city of Beer Sheva. On the eastern outskirts of the city lie the crumbling remains of one of the oldest towns on earth, Tel Beersheba, the City of the Seven Wells. There amidst its tumbled ruins archeologists had unearthed the deep bore of an ancient well, one so old that it fits the Genesis description of a well dug by the Biblical patriarch Abraham.[64] Abraham was, of course, the father of the Jewish people, but he was also considered the chief ancestor of the Arabs. It was across the mouth of this well that Anwar Sadat and Menachem Begin, virtually unnoticed by the world media, stood that day, facing each other. Then, one of them took a small piece of bread, broke it, and handed it to the other. They both ate.

And with the eating of that little piece of bread, Sadat and Begin put to rest, at least temporarily, three thousand seven hundred years of conflict...

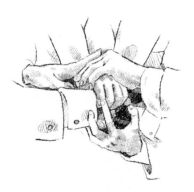

To be remembered as a peace-maker would certainly be a lasting legacy of true greatness. President Bill Clinton, seeking such a legacy, arranged for the official signing of the "Oslo Accords" to take place in Washington D.C. in September of 1993. The Oslo Accords, a product of secret negotiations held in Norway between representatives of the Palestine Liberation Organization (PLO) and Israel, were intended to create a lasting peace and a stable relationship between the two stubborn enemies. The great hope of these diplomats was to bring a permanent end to the decades-long cycle of bloody violence and revenge that divided their peoples. At President Clinton's urging, PLO President Yasser Arafat and Israeli Prime Minister Yitzhak Rabin flew to Washington to witness the signing of the celebrated document. There would finally be peace, they thought.

The ceremony was spectacular. Framed by the grand backdrop of the White House gleaming under a crisp blue sky, delegates of the PLO and Israel sat down at a splendid antique table, each in turn signing the hopeful treaty. Standing as witnesses over the great event were a handful of radiant dignitaries, including Rabin, Clinton, and Arafat. When the last pen was laid down on the polished surface of the heavy table, the signing complete and official, President Clinton proudly stood forth and presented the peacemakers to an ecstatic, cheering world. Then, an extraordinary thing happened. With a broad toothy grin, PLO president Yasser Arafat extended his hand to Prime Minister Yitzhak Rabin in an unexpected gesture of peace. Taken aback by this bold act the frowning Rabin hesitated for a split-second. Then, as the watching world held its breath, he reached around and took the hand of his staunchest opponent, and shook it vigorously. He even managed a wry smile. Swept up by the thrill of such a historic moment, even the reporters and photographers erupted in exuberant applause. Peace!

Then, all the dignitaries and delegates flew away to their happy homes, and there has been blood and fire ever since.

"But they signed a treaty! They even shook hands!" cried the world, "Why didn't it work?"

The answer is almost too simple. A signature on paper or even a handshake means little amidst the ancient customs of the churning, Middle-Eastern world. But if Rabin and Arafat had together eaten just a single piece of bread, it is likely that our world today might be a very different place...

Chapter 20

Come and Eat

Food. Besides being necessary to keep us going, if we are honest, it really is one of our favorite subjects in life. It fills us and makes children grow, it tastes good (well, most of the time) and we are grateful for it. We love restaurants and potlucks, and when we gather with friends it is almost always over a meal. Food warms us and makes us smile, it brings us together and it reconciles us when we are divided. And lest we forget, it is always a gracious provision from the sovereign hand of God.

Jesus seemed to think so, too. After His resurrection, almost every time He appeared to His disciples He ate with them. Sometimes it was to calm them down, eating in front of the panicked men in order to prove that He was not a ghost. Another time He was all but dragged into the house of some disciples for supper, where He broke bread with them and immediately vanished. But most of the time He ate with them just to eat, and that meant oneness, forgiveness, and reconciliation.

On the terrible night of His betrayal every one of Jesus' disciples deserted Him, though a few would later follow at a distance. Others plunged into doubt.[65] One of them denied Him—three times. Then Jesus died. Three days later He would beat the system, and later that evening He would come and eat with them again...

Obeying the instructions of their risen Master, the disciples finally emerged out of their stuffy little room in Jerusalem and journeyed north, back to Capernaum. It was their old home town: a busy fishing village built of black rock and plaster hugging the north shore of the Sea of Galilee, and it was also the place where Jesus had called them to follow Him. Before they left Jerusalem, Jesus told them He would go ahead of them and meet them there, but when they arrived He was nowhere to be found.

This proved too much for Peter. Since the night he denied his Master he seemed to grow increasingly despondent and bitter at his terrible failure. *I cursed and swore that I never knew Him—and to a little girl! And then I turned and there He was, bound and bruised and looking at me! How could He ever forgive me? How could I ever forgive myself?* Even Jesus' Resurrection did little to pierce Peter's gathering gloom and seemed to agitate his already turbulent thoughts. And now that he arrived back in Capernaum Jesus was not there. Peter had finally had enough.

"I'm going fishing," Peter told the other disciples. This was not to say that he was heading down to the lake to drown a few worms, hoping to feel better about things in the morning. He quit. *I'm done being a disciple—I'm through with the whole thing! I'm going back to my old job!* And the Bible tells us that seven of the other disciples joined him in his little revolt, including John.[66] But what happened next would change them all forever…

So they went out and got into the boat, but that night they caught nothing.

Early in the morning, Jesus stood on the shore, but the disciples did not realize that it was Jesus.

He called out to them, "Friends, haven't you any fish?"

"No," they answered.

He said, "Throw your net on the right side of the boat and you will find some." When they did, they were unable to haul the net in because of the large number of fish.

Then the disciple whom Jesus loved [John] said to Peter, "It is the Lord!" As soon as Simon Peter heard him say, "It is the Lord," he wrapped his outer garment around him (for he had taken it off) and jumped into the water. The other disciples followed in the boat, towing the net full of fish, for they were not far from shore, about a hundred yards. When they landed, they saw a fire of burning coals there with fish on it, and some bread.

Jesus said to them, "Bring some of the fish you have just caught."

Simon Peter climbed aboard and dragged the net ashore. It was full of large fish, 153, but even with so many the net was not torn. Jesus said to them, "Come and have breakfast." None of the disciples dared ask him, "Who are you?" They knew it was the Lord. Jesus came, took the bread and gave it to them, and did the same with the fish.[67]

Three years before, these professional fishermen had dropped their nets, tied up their boats, and turned their backs on a successful business to follow Him. Now, after their first night back at their old job their nets were dismally empty. It was the best fishing hole in the lake, yet they had caught nothing, not even a guppy, and it made perfect sense. They were supposed to be out catching men. Another failure for poor, unhappy Peter.

So it was that when Jesus finally appeared, He gave them all that they wanted and more. It was the largest single catch this company of professional fishermen had ever netted: a hundred and fifty-three large fish. And that is when they began to realize that all they ever really wanted was found in Him.

"Come and have breakfast," Jesus called to them.* And there, as the clear new rays of the morning sun bathed their battered boat and tired bodies, they wandered over and squatted down in silence next to the little charcoal fire. Then

* Though He was obviously capable of creating food, this time the Lord was merely the cook. To make bread, all He needed was a little oil, water, flour, salt, a charcoal fire, and a hot, flat rock.

He took bread and gave it to them, and He ate with them, and Peter, too. And that morning after their meal together, they all turned their backs on their nets and followed Him for the rest of their earthly lives.

Reconciled.

Enemies No More

Certainly one of the most wretched failures in the Bible involved an entire church. They were rich, healthy, and well-organized, so much so that Jesus merely stood in the way of their great success. So they pushed Him out of their church. It was then that Jesus decided to dictate a letter to them, to His church located in the shining city of Laodicea, and in it He spoke His mind.

"I know your deeds," Jesus rebuked them, "that you are neither cold nor hot. I wish you were either one or the other! So, because you are lukewarm—neither hot nor cold—I am about to spit you out of my mouth."[68] Those are terrifying words spoken by the Lord of the universe! But there was more. As Jesus concluded this chilling letter, He did something entirely unexpected: He pleaded with them. "Here I am!" He cried, "I stand at the door and knock. If anyone hears my voice and opens the door, I will come in *and eat with him*, and he with me."

"Come, let's eat together," Jesus says, and it is an invitation to a splendid feast where He is the gracious Host and you are His most welcome guest. "Come and eat," He calls, even if, like Peter, you have failed Him. Come and eat!

But you don't know what I've done! Why would God ever want me back?

"Come and eat!" He pleads.

But haven't you ever heard the old Middle Eastern proverb that sternly declares, "Never eat with your enemy?" I've made myself a vile enemy of God—I have done terrible things!

Then come and eat, for you are His enemy no more—He has made sure of it. Grab hold of these wondrous words of the Apostle Paul, and draw them in close to your heart:

"For if, when we were God's enemies, we were reconciled to Him by the death of His Son, how much more, having been reconciled, shall we be saved through His life?"[69]

Reconciled to Him? Saved? But how can this be?

The answer is so marvelously simple: Jesus Christ *is* the Bread of life, the Bread of God, His Manna from heaven. And God the Father takes this lovely Bread in His mighty hands, the Bread which is His own beloved Son, and passes it down to us *that we may eat of it and not die.* "See?" He says, "Here is my Son, and I hand Him to you. Take Him and eat Him, and if you do, we shall be reconciled, we will be *one*."

But there is more. As Paul so clearly reminded us,

"The Lord Jesus, on the night that He was betrayed, took bread, and when He had given thanks, He

Broken Bread | 167

broke it and said, 'This is my body, which is for you, do this in remembrance of Me.'"[70]

Do you see it now? The Father is offering to us His own broken bread. "Take it and eat it," He implores, "take *Him*, broken for you, and you and I will be one; and the quarrel of sin that I have had against you I will personally forget *for all eternity*."

I hope we will never again look at the ordinance of Communion in some tired, ordinary way. For framed in its radiant imagery the Lord Jesus Christ, the Great Host of the Feast, has also become its food.[71] The Bread of Life is truly our Great Reconciler.

Take and eat.

CHAPTER 21

Come to the Feast

So come to the feast, for here there are warm welcomings and humble hospitality, along with much singing and the joy of happy reunions. And the food! There is none like it anywhere, royally prepared and marvelously satisfying. And the Master of the feast—He is a magnificent Host! He will wash your feet and your hands, and bring you wine and bread.

And should your heart ever be troubled, He will break off a bite and slip it into your mouth. "I am your brother," He will whisper to you, "and I have laid down My life for you. I love you and I have forgiven you; and now I glorify you. You are My friend."

And in the starlit splendor of the cool evening, the sounds of merriment flow like new wine out of the doors and windows of the homely hall, echoing down the stony vales and across the distant seas of water and time.

Come to the feast. The table is set, the bread is warm, and the Master sits at His gate, poring over the broad horizon, eagerly awaiting the honor of your presence…

Leftovers

(APPENDICES)

The Second Sword

Now, about that sword at the Last Supper: John would most certainly have had a sword with him at the feast because tradition demanded that the man who was assigned the honor of being the bodyguard possess one. But what is more interesting is that *someone else* brought a second sword to the great Supper.

As Jesus and His disciples were preparing to leave the kataluma to go out to the Garden of Gethsemane, He reminded them how God provided for them and protected them the whole time they walked with Him. But now He told them that things were about to get rough, and that if they did not own a sword to sell an article of clothing and buy one. Jesus, of course, was not speaking literally, but the disciples once again missed the point. "See, Lord, here are *two* swords!"[72] someone proudly exclaimed, and held up the weapons, no doubt ready to rush out at His command and liberate Judea from her Roman oppressors.

The question is, who brought the other sword, and why?

It is only a guess, but the possibility is quite obvious when you think about it. At the conclusion of the Feast Jesus led His weary followers out of the room and across the Kidron Valley into a quiet, moonlit olive grove to pray. Instead, the exhausted disciples fell asleep. It was late, and the round moon stood almost directly overhead when Peter was jolted out of a deep sleep by Jesus commanding him to get up. Cruel noises and harsh whispers filled the shadows, and grim faces could be glimpsed in the pulsing flames of burning torches that now encircled them. All was confusion.

"Look, it's Judas!" Peter may have thought. "Wait, what is he doing? Why is he greeting the Master like that? Who are these men with him? Ah! What are they doing? They are attacking Him! I must do something!" And he pulled out a sword and began swinging, helplessly trying to protect his Master.

Peter may have been the man with the other sword at the Last Supper, because there in the Garden of Gethsemane *he* became the disciple who ended up protecting the host. This might also be a clue as to where Peter hoped to sit at the table that night. Of course Jesus had something better in mind...

Good old Peter.

Salt

J esus once told His disciples, "You are the salt of the earth. But if the salt loses its saltiness, how can it be made salty again? It is good for nothing except to be thrown out and trampled by men."[73] What an odd statement! Using flavorful imagery, Jesus told His disciples what they were, what they must not become, and what they would be worth to the world if they became it. But what did He mean?

Dinner is ready. "Everyone up to the table!" someone shouts, and a hungry family noisily piles in to the dining room, all smiling and rumbling with delight. There is a short, reverent silence as Grace is offered, then with a hearty "Amen!" the table roars to life. Bowls of steaming vegetables are passed and heaping plates ring with the cheerful clinking of knives and forks. Rising above the loud, contented din, a clear melodic voice is heard asking for the salt. A glass shaker full of fine, snow-white crystals bounds from hand to hand until it is eagerly seized by the asker. She tilts the shiny shaker downward over her plate and sprinkles a dash of the glittering grains on her mashed potatoes, bringing life to its starchy blandness. Ah, salt! How it brightens the character of even the most colorless cuisines.

If you were feasting with Jesus, however, you would find the salt by looking around your table for a small plate with a pile of dirt on it. Really. You see, your dinner salt would have been mined out of the bare brown crags surrounding a strange, salty lake called the Dead Sea. As it was dug out of the earth, the salt would have been mixed with dirt and other impurities left over by the great receding lake. It would often appear stained and grainy, not much different from ordinary desert soil, because in those days there was really no good way to refine it. Workers and slaves would then heap the dirty salt into baskets or sacks, where it would be hauled off on the backs of donkeys and camels to markets in far away lands. And when you would buy your salt from the local merchant, he would scoop into your basket what looked like pale dirt, or at least very dirty salt.

Now, you have tasted your food and decided that it could definitely use a little help,* but you do not want to eat anything sprinkled with polluted salt lest you crack a tooth or become ill. But you have your ways: you reach over and grab a pinch of the "dirt". Then, holding it over the salt plate, you begin to rub your thumb and fingers together. As you do, the impurities begin to fall away, back onto the plate, leaving you with a good clean pinch of salt that you discreetly sprinkle on your needy meal. And by the end of the feast all that remains on the plate is a pile of contaminated dirt.

---

* In the Middle East it is an insult to the host to salt your food before tasting it!

But that, too, was good for something, namely, *killing weeds*. If you wanted to keep weeds from popping up in certain places, like a path or a work area, you would take the leftover impurities from your plate of salt and dump them where you wanted nothing to grow. And nothing would, because the impurities in Dead Sea salt are toxic, and it would poison the soil.

"You are the salt of the earth," Jesus told His disciples. The world He made so long ago was once perfect and rich in the flavor of God's presence, and everything was good. But now, even though much of it remains lovely, it is all only an echo of Eden. Creation has been shattered and broken by sin and self-will, and it has lost much of its delicious, original flavor—the flavor of God and all His great goodness in this world. But Jesus has told His followers what they are while they are here: *You are the salt of the earth*. He has rubbed the impurities out of us and sprinkled us all over a wide world that has lost the rich full flavor of God. *You are the salt of the earth. You* bring out His savoriness among a people who have forgotten what He tastes like; *you* are the tang and zest of the world the way it was before it fell, when all was perfect and God walked with man in the Garden. Our very presence on the earth tastes of Him.

Taste and see that the LORD is good!,[74] King David rejoiced. And the LORD is tasted when we are *here*. As His followers we are called to a ministry of presence, and by just being here people can taste His goodness. Our lives have been purified just as He is pure; we bear a crop of good fruit, and it all comes from Him, because He is the vine, our source. We taste like Him, and when we are around, everything in the world tastes better because of Him. And if someone takes a bite out of us, they will taste of the One who brings out the flavor of all that was once lost, but is now made new again in His very own people. That is the way it should be, the way Jesus intended.

But then Jesus said something else: "But if the salt loses its saltiness, how can it be made salty again? It is good for nothing except to be thrown out and trampled by men."

Do you see it? How does salt lose its saltiness? When it becomes a pile of impurities. Think about it: a salty Christian is one who keeps himself pure, and in a world where morality doesn't count for much anymore, a pure person carries around a lot of flavor. But if someone who says they follow Christ decides that purity is not all that important, then according to Jesus they might still be useful for something. Killing weeds.

I think I would rather be flavorful...

But thanks be to God, who always leads us in triumphal procession in Christ and through us spreads everywhere the fragrance of the knowledge of Him. For we are to God the aroma of Christ among those who are being saved and those who are perishing.

– The Apostle Paul, 2 Corinthians 2:14-15 –

Devoted to the Breaking of Bread

There is a little verse in the Book of Acts that gives us the perfect recipe for a healthy, fruitful church: *They devoted themselves to the apostles' teaching and to the fellowship, to the breaking of bread and to prayer.*[75] A church that is devoted to the teaching of the apostles' doctrine will grow in the grace and knowledge of God. A church that is devoted to fellowship will grow in their love for one another. A church that is devoted to prayer will see God work. But a church that is devoted to the breaking of bread will be one.

We assume, of course, that *the breaking of bread* is referring to the ordinance of communion, and how the early church practiced the Lord's Supper faithfully. But if that is the case, then why does this telling verse only mention the bread and not the cup? Bible commentators are somewhat at odds with each other about this strange omission, but when you understand what the breaking of bread meant to those people (and now you do), then perhaps this particular verse is not speaking of communion at all. Perhaps the early church kept a habit of eating with each other to make sure they constantly remained *one* with each other.

As a pastor, I have often observed a sad, unnecessary, and wholly unbiblical thing occur among too many church-going Christians. Occasionally two people or even two groups who are members of a particular church will lock horns with each other. And what is their solution to the situation? One of them leaves *humbly* and *for the better* and begins attending a neighboring church down the road. But the early Christians were not able to do such things. In most towns and villages there was only one fellowship, and though there may have been several gatherings in the great cities like Ephesus or Rome, most Christians had to learn to live with each other right where they were.

In other words, changing churches because you got mad at somebody was all but impossible, and besides, Jesus did not give His followers that option. You had to do something about it. This, of course meant that you had a couple of hard choices: separate yourself permanently from the fellowship, which was not practical, or humble yourself and be reconciled with your opponent.

So the first church broke bread with each other, all the time, and they were devoted to it. They chose to humble themselves with each other and to live in a permanent state of reconciliation and brotherhood. They knew that people would have conflicts, and they willingly submitted to the great mandate of Jesus, who prayed to His Father that "they may be one as we are one: I in them and You in Me. May they be brought to complete unity *to let the world know* that You sent Me and have loved them even as You have loved Me."[76] The first church understood *exactly* what Jesus was asking of His Father on their behalf, and they also knew that He allowed no exceptions. Jesus never prayed that they be one *unless*, or *except when*, or *but*. The unity among Christians is a Divine absolute.

But there is more. At that time Jesus also prayed, "I have given them the glory that You gave Me, that they may be one as we are one..." Did you hear what He prayed? The oneness among Christian brothers and sisters is His *glory*. It is certain that most Christians want to glorify God, and we all have many different ideas as to what that looks like. But Jesus told us *exactly* what His glory is: our oneness in Him. To glorify Him is to be one with each other. And the breaking of bread reconciles us to each other and it keeps us one. This is His glory. That is why the first church was devoted to the breaking of bread. I wonder what the world would be like if the church today really believed this?

An Athenian philosopher named Aristides, observing a fellowship of early Christians, wrote:

"They abstain from all impurity in the hope of the recompense that is to come in another world. As for their servants or handmaids or children, they persuade them to become Christians by the love they have for them; and when they become so, they call them without distinction, brothers. They do not

worship strange gods; and they walk in all humility and kindness, and falsehood is not found among them; and they love one another. When they see the stranger they bring him to their homes and rejoice over him as over a true brother; for they do not call those who are after the flesh, but those who are in the Spirit and in God.

And if there is among them a man that is poor and needy and if they have not an abundance of necessities, they fast two or three days, that they may supply the needy with the necessary food.

They observe scrupulously the commandment of their Messiah; they live honestly and soberly as the Lord their God commanded them. Every morning and all hours on account of the goodness of God toward them, they render praise and laud Him over their food and their drink; they render Him thanks..."

"Such is the law of the Christians and such is their conduct."[77]

***

One last morsel of food for thought: isn't it interesting that when the Lord Jesus taught His disciples to pray, He also told them to say (in this order), "Give us today our daily bread. Forgive us our debts, as we also have forgiven our debtors..."?[78]

Hmm...

ACKNOWLEDGMENTS

A Biblical Dinner

Ahhh!" I remember hearing my friend Gayle Erwin sigh with delight as we ducked through the doorway of the ancient building. We were amazed. It was twilight in Jerusalem, we halted wide-eyed and open-mouthed in a medium-sized lamp-lit chamber that was nearly two thousand years old.

There in front of us stood two massive stone tables, angular and U-shaped, each low to the ground with thick polished tops. Stout stools and soft padded benches encircled the heavy tables, and at the back of the room a rough-hewn wooden ladder climbed into a clever loft built of sturdy branches and rope. Soft lamplight flickered on the uneven walls, and many small clay bowls full of food were set neatly on the tabletops. Neither of us could believe our eyes. It was perfect: it looked just like the *real* Last Supper.

The place was called Tantur, a round, rocky hill rising out of a disputed no-man's land between Bethlehem and Jerusalem, and it was a historian's dream. Tantur was old—

really old, and unearthed on its ragged slopes were many relics and ruins of a remote Biblical past. The wide, flat circle of a threshing floor was uncovered there, and a stone sheepfold, a watchtower, a quarry, and more, all beautifully restored and very ancient. The hill of Tantur was also the location of a modern research facility known as "Biblical Resources," a group of Bible history detectives headed up by archeology professor Dr. Jim Fleming. It was he who had restored the old building and decorated it, and he got it just right.

Several years before, I attended a pastor's conference where I had heard Gayle give an inspired message on the *historical* Last Supper of the Bible, which completely rearranged my thinking about that wonderful, notorious night. But now we found ourselves standing in it—a living, three-dimensional, *accurate* recreation of the Upper Room. "Gayle! It looks just like your talk!" I gasped. "It does!" he answered. "Now, let's see what they do with it..."

Then, squeezing into the cozy seats around the great stone slabs, the giggling children of our group ascending into the loft, we were all served a hearty feast, Bible-style. As we dined we were introduced to one of Dr. Fleming's students, a young German researcher who would walk us step by step through the events of Jesus' last and greatest night with His disciples. It was truly a tremendous event, and it soon became one of the recurring highlights of every future tour that I would lead for Gayle. Dr. Fleming had *really* done his homework.

After several visits to Biblical Resources, however, I concluded that the amazing hands-on insights into the Last Supper were just too important to leave behind in Jerusalem. My congregation *needed* to see this. But my church, which is nestled in a remote corner of Northern California, would never have the resources to uproot for a couple of weeks and visit the Holy Land. I had to find a way of bringing the Biblical Resources experience home. And with their gracious permission, I did—with one stipulation: *do your homework.*

It would have been easy to parrot Dr. Fleming's research and Gayle's rich insights to the people back home, but I had to make sure what they were saying was factual and accurate before I would ever attempt to teach it. So I started to dig in.

It was then that I made another surprising discovery: languishing on the dark shelves of musty second-hand bookshops was a significant number of out-of-print books on the subject. People had actually written about this sort of thing for a long time, but over the course of many years its study had become neglected, and it was eventually all but forgotten.

But now it was becoming to me much more than a quest for some exciting new sermon material. What was it that was so captivating about this dinner in Israel? It was far more than the revelation of some forgotten customs or a seating order around an ancient supper table that gripped my attention. The dinner gave me a glimpse into something that had never really occurred to me, namely, how the people of the Bible *thought* about the ordinary stuff of life.

The way I see the world around me springs mostly from a medieval European way of thinking about things that was handed down from my ancestors. In other words, I have a Westernized mind, a way of thinking that has been heavily influenced by Greek philosophers and Renaissance art, all swimming around in a sea of modern trends. But the people of the Bible had an entirely different way of looking at life and relationships. Their thinking was Eastern and ancient, and it was poles apart from my own.

As I began plowing through books and research papers, I made yet another startling discovery: I found that, in a manner of speaking, it was possible to crawl inside the mind of a person who lived thousands of years ago in a strange part of the world and begin to see life as they saw it. And when I started looking at the Bible through a different set of eyes—*their* eyes, its miraculous content suddenly burst into a colorful three-dimensional painting, like an enormous pop-up book. Every page became an artist's canvas, a richly textured background upon which was painted all the great acts of the Bible. And most reassuring of all, none of it altered Biblical doctrine (otherwise it would be heresy) as it brought the ancient world and the Scriptures into sharper focus. When I understood the possibilities, especially as a Bible teacher, I knew what I would be doing with the rest of my life.

This was the birth of The Biblical Dinner: a vivid, edible sermon, a movable feast which I have had the privilege of sharing all over the world, an event that sprang from the brilliant presentation outline of Dr. Jim Fleming and from

Gayle Erwin's breathtaking insights into the nature of Jesus. And it was the beginning of this book as well, which is (hopefully) a fulfillment of the requests of so many good friends.

Dr. Fleming and Gayle are on virtually every page of this book, as are a great many other superb Bible detectives. To these men and women I offer my heartfelt thanks, for you have blessed many more than you will ever know this side of heaven.

JAY McCARL

SELECTED BIBLIOGRAPHY

Arnold, Clinton E. *Zondervan Illustrated Bible Backgrounds Commentary*. Grand Rapids, MI: Zondervan, 2002

Bailey, Kenneth E. *Jesus Through Middle Eastern Eyes: Cultural Studies in the Gospels*. Downers Grove, IL: InterVarsity Press, 2008

Bailey, Kenneth E. *Poet and Peasant*. Grand Rapids, MI: Wm. B. Eerdmans Publishing Co., 1976

Bailey, Kenneth E. *Through Peasant's Eyes*. Grand Rapids, MI: Wm. B. Eerdmans Publishing Co., 1980

Berman, Joshua. *The Temple: Its Symbolism and Meaning Then and Now*. Jason Aaronson, Inc., Northvale, New Jersey, London, 1995

Bowen, Barbara M. *Strange Scriptures that Perplex the Western Mind*. Grand Rapids, MI: Wm. B. Eerdmans Publishing Co., 1940

Chill, Abraham. *The Minhagim: The Customs and Ceremonies of Judaism, Their Origins and Rationale*. New York, NY: Sepher-Hermon Press, Inc., 1979

Connolly, Peter. *The Jews in the Time of Jesus*. Oxford: Oxford University Press, 1983

Cross, Frank Moore.* *From Epic to Canon: History and Literature in Ancient Israel*. Baltimore, MD: Johns Hopkins University Press, 1998

Daniel-Rops, Henri. *Daily Life in the Time of Jesus*. New York, NY: Hawthorn Books, Inc., New York, 1962

* This author, though a laudable scholar, espouses the Documentary Hypothesis, a theory that rejects the idea of miracles and the inspiration of the Scriptures, and with which I thoroughly disagree.

De Vaux, Roland. *Ancient Israel.* Grand Rapids, MI: Wm. B. Eerdmans Publishing Company, 1997

Edersheim, Alfred. *The Life and Times of Jesus the Messiah.* Grand Rapids, MI: Wm. B. Eerdmans Publishing Co., 1972

Edersheim, Alfred, *Sketches in Jewish Social Life in the Days of Christ*, Grand Rapids, MI: Wm. B. Eerdmans Publishing Co., 1967

Erwin, Gayle D. *The Jesus Style.* Cathedral City, CA: Yahshua Publishing, 1983

Erwin, Gayle D. *The Father Style: A fresh look at the nature of God the Father*. Cathedral City, CA: Yahshua Publishing, 1994

Erwin, Gayle D. Video lecture, *The Last Supper*. Cathedral City, CA: Yahshua Publishing

Feely-Harnik, Gillian. *The Lord's Table: The Meaning of Food in Early Judaism and Christianity*. Washington DC: Smithsonian Books, 1994

Fleming, James, Ed.D. *The World of the Bible Gardens.* Biblical Resources, Jerusalem, Israel, 1999

Fleming, James, Ed.D. *Survey of the Life of Jesus.* Biblical Resources, Jerusalem, Israel, 1990

Fleming, James, Ed.D. *Jesus in Jerusalem*. Biblical Resources, Jerusalem, Israel, 1990

Fleming, James, Ed.D. *Passover and the Last Supper.* Biblical Resources, Jerusalem, Israel, 1990

Greenberg, Rabbi Irving. *The Jewish Way: Living the Holidays*. New York, NY: Simon & Schuster, 1988

Josephus. *Antiquities of the Jews* and *The Wars of the Jews*. T.R. Whiston, translator, Grand Rapids, MI: Kregel Publications, 1960

Juster, Daniel. *Jewish Roots: A Foundation of Biblical Theology for Messianic Judaism*. Rockville, MD: DAVAR Publishing, 1986

Kasdan, Barney. *God's Appointed Customs*. Baltimore, MD: Messianic Jewish Publishers,1998

Kasdan, Barney. *God's Appointed Times*. Baltimore, MD: Messianic Jewish Publishers, 1998

King, Philip J. and Lawrence E. Stager. *Life in Biblical Israel*. Louisville, KY: Westminster John Knox Press, 2001

Knight, George W. *The Illustrated Guide to Bible Customs and Curiosities*. Uhrichsville, OH: Barbour Publishing, 2007

Kolach, Alfred J. *The Jewish Book of Why*. Jonathan David Publishers, 1995

Nun, Mendel. *The Sea of Galilee and Its Fishermen in the New Testament*. Israel: Kibbutz En Gev, 1989

Pinto, Hannaniah and James W. Fleming, Ed.D. *Jesus' Last Night with His Disciples*. Biblical Resources, LLC, 2008

Punton, Anne, *The World Jesus Knew,* Moody Press, 1996

Pritchard, James B. *The Ancient Near East: An Anthology of Texts and Pictures, Israel.* Princeton University Press, 1958

Probert, Robert. *I Am My Beloved's*. Colton, CA: Sherea Press Publishing, 1992

Rice, Edwin Wilbur. *Orientalisms in Bible Lands*. American Sunday School Union, 1910

Sacks, Stuart, *Hebrews Through a Hebrew's Eyes: Hope in the Midst of a Hopeless World*. Lederer Book, a division of Messianic Jewish Publishers, 1995

Spangler, Ann and Lois Tverber. *Sitting at the Feet of Rabbi Jesus: How the Jewishness of Jesus Can Transform Your Faith*. Grand Rapids, MI: Zondervan, 2009

Stern, David H. *The Jewish New Testament Commentary*. Baltimore: Messianic Jewish Resources International, 1992

Stern, Daniel H. *The Jewish New Testament Commentary*.
Messianic Jewish Resources International, 1992

Unterman, Alan. *Dictionary of Jewish Lore and Legend*.
Thames and Hudson Ltd., London, 1991

Vamosh, Miriam Feinberg. *Daily Life at the Time of Jesus*.
Herzila, Israel: Palphot Ltd. 1999

Vamosh, Miriam Feinberg. *Food at the Time of the Bible*.
Herzila, Israel: Palphot Ltd., 2004

Vamosh, Miriam Feinberg. *Women at the Time of the Bible*.
Herzila, Israel: Palphot Ltd., 2007

Wagner, Jr., Clarence H. *Lessons from the Land of the Bible*.
Israel: Bridges for Peace, 1998

Wight, Fred H. *Manners and Customs of Bible Lands*.
Chicago: Moody Press, 1953

END NOTES

1   Portrait of John Tait of Harvieston, 1790's, by Sir Henry Raeburn, British Art of the 18th and 19th Centuries, Section 13, Item 18. A gift of Richard B. Gump to the California Palace of the Legion of Honor, San Francisco, California.
2   John 14:8-11
3   Numbers 6:24-26
4   Luke 10:3,4
5   Philippians 2:3
6   Philippians 2:6-9
7   Matthew 10:39
8   Matthew, Chapters 5 through 7
9   Romans 16:16, 1 Corinthians 16:20, 2 Corinthians 13:12, 1 Thessalonians 5:26, 1 Peter 5:14
10   John 13:35
11   John 17:12
12   John 13:35
13   Acts 11:26
14   1 Peter 4:9
15   John 13:18
16   Matthew 10:40-42
17   John 4:7-42
18   Luke 15:8-10
19   Luke 22:7-13
20   Suggested by Dr. Jim Fleming
21   Luke 7:40-50
22   Matthew 15:2
23   Psalm 24:4
24   Romans 3:23
25   Matthew 6:7
26   Matthew 14:19
27   John 17:1
28   John 2:1-11
29   Haim Shapiro, from an article in the Jerusalem Post, *Showing Bread at the Yishuv Museum*, January 17, 2003
30   Biblical Resources, suggested from the Biblical Meal presentation by Dr. Jim Fleming
31   John 6:32-33
32   John 6:48-51

33   John 6:66
34   Luke 6:9-10
35   Matthew 25:34-40
36   Psalm 16:11
37   Acts 20:35
38   Galatians 6:7
39   Isaiah 25:6
40   Matthew 20:20-24
41   Luke 14:8-11
42   Matthew 20:25-28
43   John 13:13
44   Matthew 26:21a, Mark 14:18, Luke 22:21, John 13:21
45   Matthew 26:26-28, Mark 14:22-24, Luke 22:17-20, 1 Corinthians
     11:23-25,
46   John 13:22-25
47   John 21:20
48   Mark 14:18
49   John 13:21-26
50   John 17:12
51   2 Thessalonians 2:3
52   John 13:27-30
53   Matthew 5:43-44
54   Luke 6:27
55   Matthew 5:47
56   Romans 5:10
57   Romans 5:8
58   John 13:6-8a
59   Matthew 16:16-17
60   John 13:8-9
61   Philippians 2:6-11
62   John 13:12-17
63   Matthew 20:25-28
64   Genesis 21:30-31
65   Matthew 28:17
66   John 21:1-3
67   John 21:3-13
68   Revelation 3:15-16
69   Romans 5:10
70   1 Corinthians 11:23-24
71   Suggested by Dr. Peter Kreeft; from the lecture, "Shocking Beauty",
     2007
72   Luke 22:35-38
73   Matthew 5:13

74   Psalm 34:8
75   Acts 2:42
76   John 17:22-23
77   The Apology of Aristides, A.D. 120-130 Syriac text and translation. Cited in Encyclopedia Britannica, Vol. 1 (Chicago Encyclopedia Britannica, Inc.), p. 346
78   Matthew 6:11-12

Additional writings and resources by Jay, including information about having a Biblical Dinner presentation with your church or organization, are available through:

Web site: www.biblicaldinners.org

Email: *jay@biblicaldinners.org*

Mailing address:
Biblical Dinners, P.O. Box 111
Greenwood, CA 95635-0111

Or call toll free: 1-800-240-0927